CYCLE FOOD

A GUIDE TO SATISFYING
YOUR INNER TUBE

Written and Illustrated
by
Lauren Hefferon

Ten Speed Press
Berkeley, California

✳ THIS BOOK IS DEDICATED WITH LOVE TO MAMA ORAZIETTI
THE WOMAN WHO FIRST SATISFIED MY INNER TUBE
AND DAD FOR PRESENTING ME WITH MY FIRST
RED TRICYCLE ✳

TEN SPEED PRESS
P O Box 7123
Berkeley, California 94707

You may order single copies prepaid direct from the publisher for $4.95 + $1.00 for
postage and handling (California residents add 6% state sales tax; Bay Area residents
add 6½%).

Library of Congress Catalog Number: 83-40023
ISBN: 0-89815-099-X

Book and Cover Design by Lauren Hefferon

Printed in the United States of America

10 9 8 7 6 5 4 3 2 1

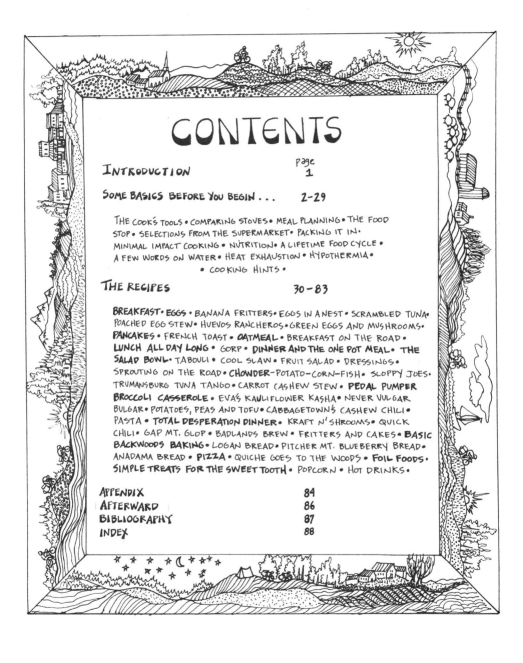

CONTENTS

ACKNOWLEDGEMENTS

FEW PEOPLE HAVE INFLUENCED MY LIFE AS **PETER KAHN** HAS — ARTIST, WRITER, PHILOSOPHER, TEACHER, GOURMET COOK AND VOLUNTEER FIREMAN — THROUGH EXAMPLE, HE INSPIRES HIS STUDENTS TO LIVE THEIR LIFE IN TUNE WITH AN ART SPIRIT RATHER THAN MERELY AS PRODUCERS OF "FINE ART."

I AM GRATEFUL TO PETER NOT ONLY FOR SHARING HIS UNIQUE ARTISTIC VISION WITH ME, BUT FOR INTRODUCING ME TO A KIND OF LEARNING THAT EXTENDS BEYOND THE CLASSROOM OR TEXTBOOK. THANK-YOU PETER FOR YOUR ENCOURAGEMENT IN THIS ATTEMPT TO FUSE MY PASSIONS FOR BICYCLING, COOKING AND THE VISUAL ARTS.

I WOULD ALSO LIKE TO OFFER A WARM THANKS TO: **CAROL KALAFATIC,** FOR HER SENSITIVE CRITICISM AND EDITING OF MY TEXT; "**LINDINO**" COPMAN," WHOSE EMOTIONAL STRENGTH IS ALWAYS REVITALIZING; **NEO MARTINEZ,** WHO SHARED HIS WISDOM AND EXPERIENCE ON COOKING EQUIPMENT AND CONTRIBUTED THE MAJORITY OF THE INFORMATION ON STOVES; **THE GANG AT** 109 VALENTINE FOR THEIR SUPPORT THROUGHOUT THE PROGRESS OF THIS BOOK; AND ALL MY **SPECIAL FRIENDS** WHO HAVE OFFERED THEIR CULINARY SUGGESTIONS, AND WHO SHARE WITH ME A CONTINUAL INTEREST IN THE ART OF "SATISFYING YOUR INNER TUBE;" FINALLY I AM FOREVER INDEBTED TO MY **BLUE FUJI** FOR ITS LOYALTY AND ABILITY TO WHET MY APPETITE AS NOTHING ELSE HAS.

TRAVELING BY ONE'S OWN POWER IS CONDUCIVE TO A ROARING APPETITE AND ANYONE WHO HAS VENTURED OUT BACKPACKING FOR MILES THROUGH THE COUNTRYSIDE KNOWS HOW A WARM MEAL CAN SATISFY BOTH THE TUMMY AND THE SOUL. CARRYING, PREPARING AND FINALLY SAVORING A MEAL IN THE WILDERNESS REINFORCES OUR ABILITY TO BE SELF-SUFFICIENT CREATURES. AWAY FROM THE LUXURIES OF A SOFT BED AND A REFRIGERATOR WE ARE REMINDED OF OUR PLACE IN THE LIFE "CYCLE" THAT REQUIRES ONLY THAT WE SLEEP WHEN TIRED AND EAT WHEN HUNGRY.

THAT STEAMING BOWL OF MUSH MIGHT APPALL THE FINEST GOURMET COOK, BUT ITS CONTENTS FILL THE VOID HOLLOWED OUT BY PHYSICAL CHALLENGES. IF PREPARED SIMPLY, CREATIVELY, AND AS A SOCIAL ACTIVITY, THAT MUSH CAN METAMORPHIZE INTO THE GRAND FINALE (OR BEGINNING) OF AN ADVENTUROUS DAY. THIS LITTLE COOKBOOK IS A GUIDE FOR THE BICYCLE TOURIST AND OTHER TRAVELERS WHO WANT TO ENJOY NUTRITIOUS, SATISFYING MEALS THAT DON'T SIMPLY SUPPLEMENT ONE'S TRAVELS, BUT ENRICH THEIR MEANING.

The Cook's Tools

PART OF WHAT I ENJOY ABOUT COOKING OUTDOORS IS DOING WITHOUT DRAWERS AND CABINETS FULL OF POTS AND PANS — IT MAKES CLEANING SO MUCH EASIER! KEEPING COOKING GEAR TO A MINIMUM IS _ESSENTIAL_, FOR IT REDUCES WEIGHT AND SIMPLIFIES MEALS. YOU DON'T HAVE TO SPEND A FORTUNE ON A FANCY COOK KIT, ALTHOUGH YOUR EQUIPMENT SHOULD BE OF GOOD ENOUGH QUALITY TO WITHSTAND SOME ABUSE (LIKE FALLING OFF YOUR BIKE). IF YOU'RE TRYING TO CUT COSTS — CHECK OUT ARMY SURPLUS STORES OR TAG SALES FOR LIGHTWEIGHT, DURABLE COOKING GEAR: I RECOMMEND THE FOLLOWING EQUIPMENT FOR A GROUP OF SIX:

THE BASICS:

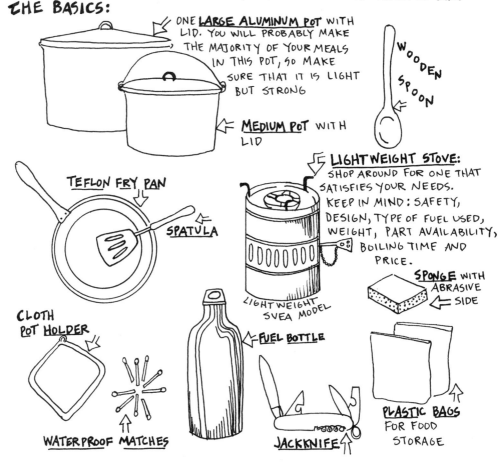

ONE **LARGE ALUMINUM POT** WITH LID. YOU WILL PROBABLY MAKE THE MAJORITY OF YOUR MEALS IN THIS POT, SO MAKE SURE THAT IT IS LIGHT BUT STRONG

WOODEN SPOON

MEDIUM POT WITH LID

TEFLON FRY PAN

SPATULA

LIGHTWEIGHT STOVE: SHOP AROUND FOR ONE THAT SATISFIES YOUR NEEDS. KEEP IN MIND: SAFETY, DESIGN, TYPE OF FUEL USED, WEIGHT, PART AVAILABILITY, BOILING TIME AND PRICE.

LIGHTWEIGHT SVEA MODEL

SPONGE WITH ABRASIVE SIDE

CLOTH POT HOLDER

FUEL BOTTLE

PLASTIC BAGS FOR FOOD STORAGE

WATERPROOF MATCHES

JACKKNIFE

2.

HELPFUL EXTRAS:

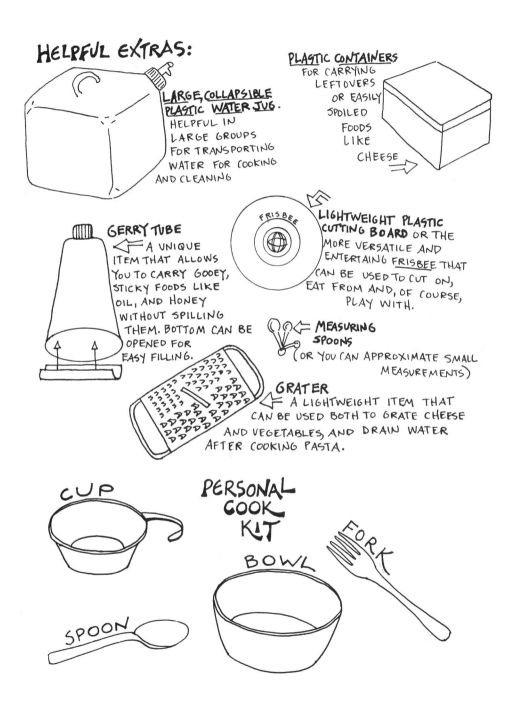

LARGE, COLLAPSIBLE PLASTIC WATER JUG.
HELPFUL IN LARGE GROUPS FOR TRANSPORTING WATER FOR COOKING AND CLEANING

PLASTIC CONTAINERS
FOR CARRYING LEFTOVERS OR EASILY SPOILED FOODS LIKE CHEESE

GERRY TUBE
A UNIQUE ITEM THAT ALLOWS YOU TO CARRY GOOEY, STICKY FOODS LIKE OIL, AND HONEY WITHOUT SPILLING THEM. BOTTOM CAN BE OPENED FOR EASY FILLING.

FRISBEE

LIGHTWEIGHT PLASTIC CUTTING BOARD OR THE MORE VERSATILE AND ENTERTAINING FRISBEE THAT CAN BE USED TO CUT ON, EAT FROM AND, OF COURSE, PLAY WITH.

MEASURING SPOONS
(OR YOU CAN APPROXIMATE SMALL MEASUREMENTS)

GRATER
A LIGHTWEIGHT ITEM THAT CAN BE USED BOTH TO GRATE CHEESE AND VEGETABLES, AND DRAIN WATER AFTER COOKING PASTA.

CUP

PERSONAL COOK KIT

FORK

BOWL

SPOON

The Spice Kit

AN ESSENTIAL PART OF MY COOKING GEAR IS A SPICE KIT, FOR ITS CONTENTS CAN TRANSFORM A BLAND MACARONI-GLUE STEW INTO AN APPETIZING CONCOCTION. I CARRY THE FOLLOWING SEASONINGS IN SMALL, LABELLED, FILM CANISTERS:

* CINNAMON * DILL WEED
* NUTMEG * SALT
* CUMIN * PEPPER
* OREGANO * PARSLEY
* BASIL * GARLIC POWDER
* CARAWAY * CHILI POWDER
* CURRY POWDER * SOY SAUCE

COMPLEMENTARY SEASONINGS

CURRY POWDER * GINGER * GARLIC * BLACK PEPPER ⟩ VEGETABLE STIR FRYS

CHILI POWDER * BASIL * CUMIN * BLACK PEPPER ⟩ CHILI, MEXICAN DISHES, BEAN DISHES.

BASIL * OREGANO * GARLIC * PARSLEY ⟩ TOMATO, EGG, CHEESE AND FISH DISHES.

CINNAMON * NUTMEG * GINGER ⟩ HOT BEVERAGES, SWEET BREADS, FRUIT SALAD.

CARAWAY * DILL WEED * PARSLEY * BLACK PEPPER ⟩ CABBAGE, CARROTS, POTATOES, SOUPS.

GARLIC * GINGER * SOY SAUCE ⟩ VEGETABLE STEWS * RICE DISHES

KEEPING IT CLEAN!

IT IS IMPORTANT TO KEEP YOUR POTS AND UTENSILS CLEAN IN ORDER TO PREVENT NASTY BACTERIA FROM MULTIPLYING IN LEFTOVER FOOD PARTICLES, WHICH CAN EVENTUALLY INFECT YOUR STOMACH. BECAUSE SOAP CAN LEAVE A FILM ON YOUR DISHES AND CAUSE DIARRHEA, ITS USE SHOULD BE ELIMINATED OR MINIMIZED. MAKE SURE TO WASH AND RINSE ALL YOUR POTS AND PANS AFTER EACH MEAL, AND STERILIZE THEM EVERY FEW DAYS IN A POT OF BOILING WATER. SHARING OF UTENSILS MIGHT SEEM A PART OF THE GROUP SPIRIT, BUT IT OFTEN JUST RESULTS IN A COMMUNAL COLD OR DIARRHEA

Comparing Stoves

A RELIABLE, LIGHTWEIGHT STOVE IS CRUCIAL FOR THE CYCLIST WHO OFTEN CAMPS WHERE FIRES ARE FORBIDDEN OR IMPRACTIBLE (i.e. PRIVATE CAMP-GROUNDS, NEAR HEAVILY USED ROADS, OR ON PRIVATE LAND) BELOW IS A CHART WITH A RUN-DOWN ON THE 5 MOST POPULAR, LIGHTWEIGHT CAMPING STOVES.

MAKE and MODEL	FUEL	EMPTY WEIGHT	FULL WEIGHT	FUEL CAPACITY	approximate BOILING TIME	approximate BURN TIME	FEATURES
COLEMAN PEAK 1	WHITE GAS	28 ounces	36.5 ounces	11.8 ounces	3½ min.	3 hr. 30 min.	PUMP, WIND-SCREEN, FOLD OUT LEGS
MSR-X-GK	MULTI-FUEL	16 ounces	DEPENDS ON FUEL	22 ounces	DEPENDS ON FUEL	DEPENDS ON FUEL	PUMP, WIND-SCREEN, HEAT REFLECTOR
HANK ROBERTS MINI MARK III	BUTANE	7.8 ounces	17 ounces	6.2 ounces	5½ min.	1 hr 30 min	WINDSCREEN
SVEA 123R	WHITE GAS	19½ ounces	22 ounces	4½ ounces	6½ min.	1 hr.	COOKPOT, WINDSCREEN
CAMPING GAZ S200S	BUTANE	10 ounces	16 ounces	6¾ ounces	8-10 min	1 hr.	ADJUSTABLE STAINLESS ARMS.

"WE'VE COME A LONG WAY SINCE OUR ANCESTORS FIGURED OUT HOW TO RUB STICKS TO WARM UP WHATEVER CARCASS HAPPENED TO MAKE IT TO THE PRIMORDIAL CAMP SITE. 20th CENTURY CAMPSTOVES ARE NOW DEPENDABLE, CONTROLLABLE AND ABLE TO PLEASE THE MOST PICKY GOURMET. OF COURSE EACH STOVE HAS ITS LIMITS AND UNIQUE APPLICATIONS, BUT WE HAVE A WIDE VARIETY OF IMPRESSIVELY APPROPRIATE STOVES TO CHOOSE FROM. AT LEAST THEY ARE INFINITELY PREFERABLE TO RUBBING STICKS"

— **NEO MARTINEZ** — OWNER AND USER OF 7 CAMP STOVES

FIVE POPULAR AND RELIABLE ALTERNATIVES TO RUBBING TWO STICKS TOGETHER:

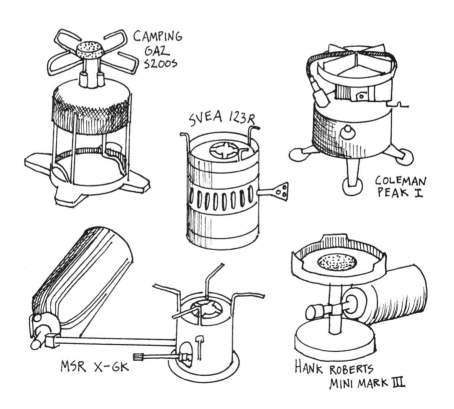

CAMPING GAZ S200S

SVEA 123R

COLEMAN PEAK I

MSR X-GK

HANK ROBERTS MINI MARK III

BEFORE YOU SPEND ALOT OF MONEY ON A STOVE, IT IS WISE TO WEIGH THE ADVANTAGES AND DISADVANTAGES OF SEVERAL MODELS. THEN CHOOSE THE STOVE THAT WILL BEST SATISFY YOUR NEEDS AND PERSONAL PREFERENCE.

MAKE and MODEL	ADVANTAGES	DISADVANTAGES
COLEMAN PEAK I	• GREAT FLAME CONTROL • STABLE • GOOD WIND SCREEN • LARGE FUEL CAPACITY • HIGH HEAT OUTPUT • • GOOD FLAME SPREAD •	HEAVY • BURNS ONLY WHITE GAS • • BURNS DIRTY WITH UNLEADED GAS • • BULKY •
MSR-G/K	• MULTI-FUEL (WHITE GAS, DIESEL FUEL, HEATING OIL, KEROSENE) • LIGHT • HIGH HEAT OUTPUT • • HUGE FUEL CAPACITY • COMPACT • STABLE • PUMP AND FLINT FLAME STARTER – EASY TO LIGHT •	• POOR FLAME CONTROL • ASSEMBLY AND DISASSEMBLY REQUIRED BEFORE AND AFTER EACH USE • EXPENSIVE • POOR FLAME SPREAD • AWKWARD WIND SCREEN •
HANK ROBERTS	• LIGHT • COMPACT • EASY TO START • • PROPANE CARTRIDGES DISCON- NECTABLE • FUNCTIONS BEST OF ANY GAS CARTRIDGE STOVE IN COLD WEATHER • GOOD FLAME SPREAD • OPTIONAL LANTERN KIT •	• POOR FUEL AVAILABILITY • FUEL IS EXPENSIVE AND HAS MODERATE HEAT OUTPUT • CARTRIDGE VALVE OFTEN GETS STUCK •
SVEA 123R	• VERY DURABLE • DEPENDABLE • • LIGHT • COMPACT • EASILY ASSEMBLED AND DISASSEMBLED IN THE FIELD • " A TOUGH LITTLE CHUGGER "	• POOR FLAME CONTROL • POOR FLAME SPREAD • MODERATE HEAT OUTPUT • SMALL FUEL CAPACITY • NOISY • DANGEROUS PRIMING NECESSARY • UNSTABLE
CAMPING GAZ 5200S	LIGHT • INEXPENSIVE • EASY TO OPERATE • RELIABLE •	POOR FUEL AVAILABILITY • HIGH FUEL EXPENSE • POOR HEAT OUTPUT IN COLD • LOW HEAT OUTPUT IN WARM • NONDISEN- GAGABLE FUEL CARTRIDGE •

Meal Planning

UNLIKE THE BACKPACKER WHO HAS TO CARRY ALL THE FOOD FOR HIS TRIP, THE BIKE TOURER REPLENISHES HIS SUPPLY DAILY AT GENERAL STORES, SUPERMARKETS, OR NATURAL FOOD STORES. THE MAIN ADVANTAGE IS THAT THE CYCLE TOURIST USUALLY HAS A WIDER SELECTION OF FRESH FOODS TO CHOOSE FROM THAN THE BACKPACKER, WHO OFTEN HAS TO DEPEND MORE ON DRIED OR FREEZE-DRIED RATIONS.

AFTER CYCLING FOR MILES, THERE IS NOTHING LIKE STOPPING AT A ROADSIDE STAND THAT ABOUNDS IN THIRST-QUENCHING FRUITS OR CRUNCHY VEGETABLES. YOUR DIET, HOWEVER, OFTEN DEPENDS UPON WHAT'S AVAILABLE IN THE AREA YOU TRAVEL THROUGH. WHILE TOURING THE COAST OF MAINE, WE INDULGED IN THE ABUNDANT SEAFOOD OF THE AREA. BUT WHEN WE HIT THE DESOLATE COAST OF NOVA SCOTIA, OUR DIET WAS OFTEN LIMITED TO CANNED AND DRIED RATIONS. BE PREPARED TO ACCOMODATE YOUR MEALS TO WHATEVER IS AVAILABLE IN SMALL COUNTRY STORES. WHEN PLANNING YOUR TRIP, CONSIDER THE FOLLOWING:

TOURING STYLE:

- CAMPER TOURIST — IS THE MODE OF TOURING I ADVOCATE; BY CARRYING YOUR OWN HOME AND FOOD, YOU AND YOUR BICYCLE ARE A SELF-SUFFICIENT TEAM.

- LIGHT TOURIST — IF YOU DO NOT WANT TO BE BOTHERED WITH CARRYING CAMPING EQUIPMENT, CONSIDER SLEEPING IN HOTELS OR HOSTELS AND EATING IN RESTAURANTS. WHILE THIS MAY BE LESS CUMBERSOME, PLAN ON SPENDING AT LEAST 3 TIMES AS MUCH AS THE CAMPER TOURIST.

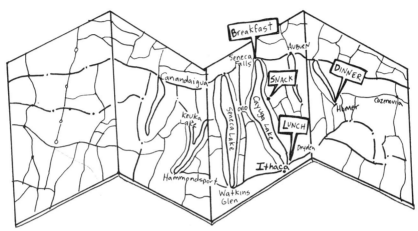

- <u>HOSTELER TOURIST</u> — THIS IS A COMBINATION OF THE CAMPER TOURIST AND THE LIGHT TOURIST WHO SLEEPS IN HOSTELS AND EATS MOST OF THEIR MEALS IN RESTAURANTS, BUT ALSO CARRIES A LIGHTWEIGHT TENT, AND COOKING EQUIPMENT FOR OCCASIONAL CAMPING.
- <u>ORGANIZED TOURS</u> — ARE BECOMING A POPULAR WAY FOR PEOPLE OF ALL AGES TO EXPERIENCE BICYCLE TOURING. BICYCLE ROUTE ITINERARIES ARE PREPLANNED, AND COSTS USUALLY INCLUDE FOOD AND SOME GROUP EQUIPMENT.

<u>LENGTH OF TRIP</u>:
- HOW OFTEN WILL YOU HAVE TO REPLENISH STAPLES? IT IS WISE TO EXAMINE YOUR ROUTE EACH MORNING SO YOU KNOW WHERE YOU CAN BUY FOOD FOR EACH MEAL.
- HOW MUCH COOKING GEAR WILL YOU NEED?
- LONG RIDING DAYS? SOMEDAYS YOU WILL PROBABLY FIND YOURSELF ON THE ROAD UNTIL LATE IN THE AFTERNOON AND WILL HAVE LITTLE TIME OR ENERGY TO PREPARE INVOLVED MEALS. SCRAMBLED EGGS, SPAGHETTI, CANNED SOUPS AND SANDWICHES ARE SATISFYING TIME SAVERS.
- SHORT DAYS? I TRY TO START MY TOURING EARLY IN THE MORNING WHEN THE TEMPERATURE IS COOL AND THE TRAFFIC IS LIGHT. ALSO, THE MORE MILEAGE I GET IN BEFORE LUNCH, THE EARLIER I CAN GET INTO CAMP AND RELAX, NAP, EXPLORE AND COOK A GOOD DINNER AT A LEISURELY PACE.

<u>CLIMATE</u>: PERISHABLES SPOIL QUICKLY IN HOT WEATHER. EXTREME WEATHER CONDITIONS (COLD, HEAT, HEAVY RAINS, OR WINDS) DEMAND A HIGHER CALORIE DIET.

NUMBER OF PEOPLE: THE MORE PEOPLE IN YOUR GROUP MEANS NOT ONLY BUYING MORE FOOD, BUT IT ALSO REQUIRES MORE VARIETY AND TOLERANCE FOR SPECIAL TASTES.

VARIETY: CAMPING FOOD IS BEGINNING TO RISE ABOVE THE BLAND AND BORING CATEGORY INTO THE REALM OF A MORE EXCITING AND FLAVORFUL CUISINE. EVEN THE MOST MUNDANE FOOD CAN BE MADE APPEALING IF SERVED IN A VARIETY OF WAYS.

BUDGET: ONE ATTRACTION OF CYCLE TOURING IS THE MINIMAL BUDGET YOU NEED TO EAT AND SLEEP WHILE TRAVELING IN THE MOST EXOTIC OF PLACES. DEPENDING ON YOUR STYLE, YOUR FOOD BUDGET CAN BE RIGIDLY LIMITED OR EXTRAVAGANTLY EXPLOITED.

AVAILABILITY OF WATER: IF YOU ARE CYCLING THROUGH POPULATED AREAS, THERE IS LITTLE CONCERN FOR RUNNING OUT OF WATER. PEOPLE ARE USUALLY MORE THAN WILLING TO FILL UP YOUR WATER BOTTLE FROM THEIR TAP. BUT IF YOU PLAN TO TRAVEL THROUGH DESOLATE OR ARID TERRAIN, I RECOMMEND THAT YOU RATION YOUR WATER SUPPLY AND CARRY AT LEAST TWO FULL WATER BOTTLES ON YOUR BIKE AND A CONTAINER OF WATER IN YOUR PACK.

EMERGENCY RATIONS: IN A CORNER OF YOUR PACK, ALWAYS CARRY AN EMERGENCY FOOD SUPPLY. IN A SEALED PLASTIC BAG, CARRY FOODS THAT WILL KEEP WELL FOR A LONG PERIOD OF TIME. FOR EXAMPLE: CANNED TUNA, NUTS, SOUP BOUILLON, HARD CANDY.

THE FOOD STOP

MOST FOOD STOPS ARE NOT ONLY ENERGY BOOSTERS, BUT GREAT OPPORTUNITIES FOR THE CYCLIST TO EXPLORE LOCAL CULTURE. THE GROCER DOES NOT ONLY SELL FOOD, HE MAY BE A SOURCE OF VALUABLE INFORMATION SUCH AS DIRECTIONS TO THE BEST SWIMMING HOLE OR OPEN FIELD FOR CAMPING.

GETTING THE BEST AND MOST FOR YOUR MONEY IS THE GOAL FOR ANY SMART SHOPPER. THE DECISIONS ON WHAT TO BUY, WHERE TO SHOP AND WHO SHOULD BUY THE FOOD INVOLVES CONSCIENTIOUS DECISIONS OF THE WHOLE GROUP.

  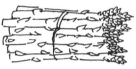

• **MAKE A SHOPPING LIST**: BEFORE YOUR GROUP OF SWEATY, TIRED AND HUNGRY CYCLISTS INVADE A SMALL COUNTRY STORE, KNOW EXACTLY WHAT AND HOW MUCH YOU NEED – REMEMBER THAT YOUR EYES ARE OFTEN BIGGER THAN YOUR STOMACH. HAVE A COUPLE PEOPLE, RATHER THAN THE WHOLE GROUP, DO THE ACTUAL SHOPPING.

• **TAKE ADVANTAGE OF ALL FOOD SOURCES AVAILABLE**:

• **NATURAL FOOD STORES**: ARE NOT AS COMMON AS SUPERMARKETS, SO WHEN YOU FIND THEM IT IS A GOOD IDEA TO STOCK UP ON BULK STAPLES SUCH AS: POWDERED MILK, FLOUR, GRANOLA, NUTS, SOY SAUCE, PEANUT BUTTER, GRAINS, BEANS, DRIED FRUIT, PASTA AND SPICES. THE MAJOR ADVANTAGE OF NATURAL FOOD STORES IS THAT YOU CAN BUY WHOLESOME FOOD IN BULK AT CHEAP PRICES, AND PREVENT WASTEFUL PACKAGING BY REUSING PLASTIC AND PAPER CONTAINERS.

• **SUPERMARKETS**: CAN USUALLY SUPPLY YOU WITH ANYTHING YOU NEED BUT YOU USUALLY PAY MORE FOR PACKAGING AND CONVENIENCE OF PRODUCTS. ALSO MANY PREPARED AND PACKAGED FOODS HAVE ADDED PRESERVATIVES, CHEMICALS AND REFINED SUGAR WHICH YOU MAY WANT TO REDUCE IN YOUR DIET. GENERIC BRANDS OF MANY FOODS ARE OFTEN AVAILABLE AND ARE ALWAYS CHEAPER AND USUALLY IDENTICAL TO THEIR BRIGHTLY COLORED COUNTERPART. STAPLES FROM SUPERMARKETS INCLUDE: COLD CEREALS, DAIRY PRODUCTS, COFFEE, TEA, COLD DRINKS, CRACKERS, PRODUCE, CANNED AND FRESH FISH, CANNED BEANS, PASTA AND BREAD.

- **DINERS OR CAFES**: OCCASIONALLY FOR A CHANGE, I'LL TREAT MYSELF AT A DINER OR CAFE WHERE THE FOOD IS GOOD AND INEXPENSIVE. THE CASUAL ENVIRONMENT OF DINERS IS ALSO A GREAT PLACE TO MINGLE WITH THE LOCALS.
- **ROADSIDE STANDS**: WHO CAN RESIST THE FRESH AND THIRST QUENCHING PRODUCE OF LOCAL ROADSIDE STANDS — A DEFINITE FOOD STOP!!!

- **"ALL YOU CAN EAT" SPAGHETTI SUPPERS OR PANCAKE BREAKFASTS**: MAKE SURE TO CHECK OUT THE LOCAL PAPERS AND BILLBOARDS FOR "ALL YOU CAN EAT" BREAKFASTS OR DINNERS SPONSORED BY CHURCHES OR OTHER ORGANIZATIONS.

- **NICE PEOPLE WHO WANT TO ADOPT AND FEED YOU**: THIS IS PERHAPS WHAT MAKES BICYCLE TOURING SO SPECIAL. ALONG THE WAY YOU ALWAYS MEET LOTS OF NICE FOLK WHO THINK WHAT YOU ARE DOING IS SOMEHOW HEROIC, AND FEEL A NEED TO NURTURE YOUR JOURNEY BY STUFFING YOU WITH DINNER OR BREAKFAST. I LIKE TO RECIPROCATE SUCH HOSPI-TALITY BY DOING YARDWORK OR WATCHING THEIR RUNNY-NOSE KIDS. BE CAREFUL THOUGH, THE HOSPITALITY IS SOMETIMES SO GENEROUS THAT YOU DON'T WANT TO RETURN TO CANNED BEANS AND PASTA. IT'S A NICE IDEA TO FOLLOW-UP A HOMESTAY WITH A POSTCARD OR THANK-YOU LETTER.

Selections from the Supermarket

RATHER THAN THROWING ANY EDIBLE FOOD IN SIGHT INTO YOUR CART, IT IS WORTHWHILE (ECONOMICALLY AND NUTRITIONALLY) TO SPEND SOME TIME SCANNING THE AISLES MORE CAREFULLY. TO ASSIST YOU IN YOUR SHOPPING, I HAVE COMPILED A LIST OF REASONABLY WHOLESOME AND CONVENIENT FOODS AVAILABLE AT MOST SUPERMARKETS.

BREAKFAST

AUNT JEMIMA PANCAKE MIX
CARNATION INSTANT BREAKFAST
KELLOGG'S NUTRI GRAIN CEREAL
POST'S GRAPE NUTS CEREAL
WHEATENA BRAN AND WHEAT CEREAL
KRETSCHMER'S WHEAT GERM
FAMILIA SWISS
QUAKER QUICK OATS
NABISCO SHREDDED WHEAT CEREAL

LUNCH

KRAFT BARREL CHEESE
NATURE FAMILY GRANOLA BARS
STONE GROUND CRACKERS
HONEY MAID GRAHAM CRACKERS
NABISCO ZWIEBACK TOAST
PEPPERIDGE FARM SNACK BARS
SUNMAID NATURE SNACKS
TRISCUIT WHOLE WHEAT WAFERS
MANISHEWITZ WHOLE WHEAT MATZOS
V-8 JUICE
MINUTE MAID FROZEN ORANGE JUICE
FIG NEWTONS

DRINKS

CARNATION INSTANT DRY MILK
COUNTRY TIME LEMONADE MIX
LIPTON TEA
SWISS MISS HOT COCOA MIX
TANG ORANGE DRINK

DINNER

BETTY CROCKER SCALLOPED POTATOES
BETTY CROCKER HASH BROWNS
HUNGRY JACK MASHED POTATOES
KRAFT MACARONI AND CHEESE
ELBOW MACARONI
JIFFY PIZZA CRUST
RIGATONI NOODLE SHELLS

SOUPS:

LIPTON CUP-A-SOUP:
  LOTS'A NOODLES, CREAM OF MUSH-ROOM, ONION, COUNTRY STYLE VEGETABLES
PROGRESSO CANNED SOUP:
  ZUCCHINNI, CLAM CHOWDER, TOMATO SOUP, PEA SOUP, BEANS AND HAM, MINESTRONE
CAMPBELL'S SOUP:
  GREEN PEA, CHEDDAR CHEESE, NEW ENGLAND CLAM CHOWDER CREAM OF CELERY, CREAM OF MUSHROOM
RICE-A-RONI:
  SAVORY PILAF, SPANISH RICE, ORTEGA TACO DINNER
OLD EL PASO:
  SPANISH RICE, TAMALES, TOSTADA SHELLS, CHILI, PINTO BEANS, TACO SAUCE, REFRIED BEANS
DURKEE SAUCES:
  SPAGHETTI SAUCE MIX, CHEESE SAUCE MIX, SOUR CREAM MIX, ONION GRAVY MIX, CHILI SEASONING MIX

PACKING IT IN

BEFORE YOU CAN COOK AND EAT YOUR FOOD, YOU FACE THE CHALLENGE OF HOW TO PACK IT ALL IN YOUR PANNIERS EFFICIENTLY AND WITHOUT DAMAGING IT. INEVITABLY, YOU WILL FIND YOURSELF OUTSIDE A SUPERMARKET WITH BAGS OF BULKY GROCERIES THAT NEED TO BE TRANSPORTED FOR SEVERAL MILES, AND TRYING TO FIND THE SPACE FOR A HEAD OF CAULIFLOWER, A LOAF OF BREAD OR A CARTON OF EGGS SOUNDS EASIER THAN IT ACTUALLY IS. WHILE MANY OF THE BASIC PRINCIPLES FOR PACKING FOOD FOR BIKE TOURING ARE SIMILIAR TO THOSE OF BACK-PACKING, THE LIMITED SPACE OF BIKE PANNIERS AND THE NEED TO CAREFULLY BALANCE YOUR WEIGHT, INTRODUCES ADDITIONAL CONSIDERATIONS.

- **UTILIZE** <u>ALL THE SPACE</u> OF <u>YOUR PACK</u> EFFICIENTLY BY STUFFING STAPLES LIKE POWDERED MILK, RICE AND FLOUR INTO EMPTY POTS OR CONTAINERS.
- KEEP THE FOODS YOU USE FREQUENTLY IN A <u>CONVENIENT</u> PLACE IN YOUR PACK.
- IF RIDING IN A GROUP — <u>DISTRIBUTE</u> <u>ALL</u> <u>COOKING GEAR</u> AND <u>FOODSTUFF</u> EQUALLY.
- IT IS SOMETIMES WORTHWHILE TO <u>PREPACKAGE DRY MIXES</u> OF MEALS IN THE PROPER PROPORTIONS SUCH AS:
    - PANCAKE MIX • BISCUIT MIX • SOUP MIX • GRAIN CEREAL MIX •
- BEFORE STARTING A TOUR, MAKE SURE YOU WILL HAVE ENOUGH ROOM IN YOUR PANNIERS TO TRANSPORT GROUP FOOD FROM SUPERMARKET TO CAMP.

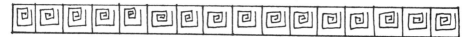

- AT THE SUPERMARKET, TRY TO REPACKAGE <u>BOXES OF FOOD</u> INTO PLASTIC BAGS. MANY PEOPLE ENJOY THE CHALLENGE OF SEEING HOW MANY FOOD ITEMS THEY CAN PILE ON TOP OF THEIR SLEEPING BAG. SUCH AN ARCHITECTURAL FEAT IS UNSAFE AND USUALLY RESULTS IN DANGLING VEGETABLES OR COMPLETELY MANGLED BREAD.

- HANDLE FRUITS, VEGETABLES, AND OTHER EASILY CRUSHED FOODS GENTLY — IT IS BEST TO CARRY FRAGILE FOODS IN THE TOP OF YOUR PANNIER COMPARTMENT. ALSO, PLACE CARTONS OF EGGS, YOGURT, COTTAGE CHEESE AND OTHER SPILLABLE FOODS INTO PLASTIC BAGS BEFORE PACKING TO SAVE YOUR GEAR IN CASE OF AN ACCIDENTAL SPILLAGE.

- <u>KNOW WHAT FOODS YOU ARE CARRYING</u>. IT IS USUALLY UNPLEASANT TO DISCOVER ROTTEN BANANAS THAT YOU FORGOT ABOUT LINING THE BOTTOM OF YOUR PACK; ALSO, AT MEAL TIMES IT AVOIDS A FRANTIC GROUP SEARCH FOR ESSENTIAL INGREDIENTS

- IF A SUPERMARKET IS CLOSE ENOUGH TO YOUR CAMP, HAVE A COUPLE OF PEOPLE EMPTY THEIR PACKS AT THE SITE AND RIDE TO THE STORE TO SHOP WHILE OTHERS CAN UNLOAD AND SET UP TENTS.

- MAKE SURE TO DISTRIBUTE THE WEIGHT OF FOODS EQUALLY IN BOTH SIDES OF YOUR PANNIERS.

- <u>STAPLES</u>: IN ADDITION TO THE VARIETY OF FRESH FOODS I BUY DAILY, THESE ARE THE STAPLE ITEMS WHICH I CARRY MOST FREQUENTLY:

POWDERED MILK	CORN MEAL
BROWN RICE	FLOUR
CEREALS	COFFEE, TEA
DRIED SOUP MIX	BAKING SODA
HONEY	BAKING POWDER
OIL	DRIED FRUIT
NUTS	BREAD
PEANUT BUTTER	VINEGAR

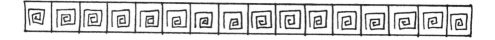

MINIMAL IMPACT COOKING

PART OF MY APPRECIATION FOR THE ENVIRONMENT AND ITS RESOURCES THAT I ENJOY SO THOROUGHLY INVOLVES PLACING A HIGH PRIORITY ON MINIMIZING MY IMPACT ON THE LAND. LEAVING A WILDERNESS AREA AS PRISTINE AS YOU FOUND IT NOT ONLY ALLOWS THE NEXT PERSON TO ENJOY IT, BUT GENERATES A SENSE OF PRIDE FOR THE ENVIRONMENT. THE PHILOSOPHY OF "MINIMAL IMPACT" IS NOT LIMITED TO THE WILDERNESS SITUATION, BUT CAN BE EXTENDED INTO A DAILY, CONSCIOUS EFFORT TO PRESERVE AND RECYCLE OUR LIMITED RESOURCES.

WHEN SETTING AND BREAKING CAMP, BE AWARE OF WHERE AND HOW YOU SET SHELTER, COOK, WASH AND RELIEVE YOURSELF.

SOME BASIC GUIDELINES OF MINIMUM IMPACT COOKING ARE:

* BAG ALL GARBAGE AND PACK IT OUT *
* NEVER WASH DISHES OR FOOD IN STREAMS OR LAKES; INSTEAD TAKE A POT OF WATER AWAY FROM STREAM OR LAKE AND WASH THEM. *
* PLAN MEALS THAT WILL BE COMPLETELY EATEN TO ELIMINATE WASTE *
* BURN OR CARRY OUT ALL LEFTOVER FOOD. *
* ELIMINATE USE OF SOAP (OR MINIMIZE); SAND AND PINENEEDLES ARE EXCELLENT ABRASIVES. *
* LIMIT USE OF FIRES — USE A STOVE FOR COOKING WHEN POSSIBLE. FIRES CAN BE HAZARDOUS, AND HAVE A LONG-TERM IMPACT ON GROUND COVER * IF FOR AESTHETIC REASONS YOU WANT TO SIT AND COOK BY A WARM, CRACKLING FIRE — TRY TO:
  * CHOOSE SITE CAREFULLY, PREFERABLY IN AN EXISTING FIREPLACE.
  * BUILD A FIRE PIT, SAVE THE SOD AND REPLACE IT AFTER, OR BUILD A FIRE ON A LARGE, FLAT ROCK.
  * KEEP FIRE SMALL
  * DOUSE FIRE COMPLETELY UNTIL YOU CAN RUN YOUR HAND THROUGH COALS AND SCATTER ASHES.

* TO ENSURE THAT ANIMALS HAVE A MINIMUM IMPACT ON YOU — ALWAYS TIE UP YOUR FOOD BEFORE GOING TO BED. COLLECT ALL UNCANNED FOOD AND HANG IT IN A STRONG BAG ON A TREE LIMB AWAY FROM ANY POSSIBLE REACH BY ANIMALS, (I HAVE SEEN SMART ALECK RACCOONS BALANCE ON MY BICYCLE IN AN EFFORT TO GET THEIR PAWS ON OUR HANGING FOOD SAC.) NEVER STORE FOOD INSIDE YOUR TENT UNLESS YOU WANT EARLY MORNING GUESTS.

THE NATIONAL OUTDOOR LEADERSHIP SCHOOL (N.O.L.S.) IS A MAJOR ADVOCATE OF MINIMAL IMPACT COOKING, HIKING AND CAMPING. THEY HAVE ESTABLISHED THE FOLLOWING GUIDELINES FOR SAFE AND MINIMAL IMPACT STOVE AND FIRE USAGE:

STOVES
- NEVER COOK INSIDE A TENT IF IT IS POSSIBLE TO COOK OUTSIDE.
- ESTABLISH A COOKING AREA AWAY FROM TENTS, BAGS AND OTHER FLAMMABLES
- BE CAREFUL WHEN POURING GASOLINE TO AVOID SPILLAGE.
- YOUR FUEL BOTTLE IS A POTENTIAL FIRE HAZARD IF LEFT OPEN OR NEAR A FLAME; BE SURE TO CAP IT TIGHTLY AFTER EACH USE.
- AFTER USING YOUR STOVE, ALLOW IT TO COOL BEFORE RELEASING THE PRESSURE
- START EACH MEAL WITH A FULL TANK
- KEEP YOUR FACE AND HAIR AWAY FROM STOVE WHEN LIGHTING.

FIRES:
DIGGING THE PIT:
- OUTLINE AREA WITH A SMALL SHOVEL, AND MAKE IT BIG ENOUGH SO FIRE WILL NOT TOUCH PERIMETER.
- CUT OUT SMALL SQUARES AND PUT THEM ASIDE. KEEP THE WATERED.
- CUT OUT ROOTS TO EDGE OF PIT. <u>MAKE SURE YOU REACH MINERAL SOIL</u> (SANDY, GRAVELLY, NO ORGANIC MATTER). DUFF (PARTIALLY DECOMPOSED ORGANIC MATTER) WILL BURN WELL, AND COULD SMOULDER AFTER A FIRE PIT IS FILLED IN, WHICH COULD RESULT IN A FOREST FIRE.
- OUTLINE PIT WITH DIRT TO PREVENT BLACKENING GRASS.
- DIG THE FIRE PIT DEEP ENOUGH TO BURY ASHES.

SOD PIECES FROM PIT: MAKE SURE TO KEEP THEM INTACT AND WATERED TO PREVENT THEM FROM DRYING OUT

REPLACE SOD SQUARES AFTER FIRE HAS BEEN PUT OUT <u>COMPLETELY</u>

BUILDING THE FIRE:
- COLLECT DEAD WOOD ONLY FROM GROUND — NEVER BREAK BRANCHES FROM A STANDING DEAD OR LIVE TREES.
- COLLECT TWIGGIES AND INCREASINGLY LARGER TWIGS, BRANCHES AND SMALL LOGS.
- LIGHT THE TWIGGIES AND PATIENTLY BUILD UP THE FIRE. MAKE THE FIRE ONLY LARGE ENOUGH TO BOIL WATER.
- KEEP ALL FLAMMABLE ITEMS AT LEAST 5 FEET FROM FIRE.
- ALWAYS WEAR SHOES AROUND FIRE AND USE POT HOLDER FOR HOT ITEMS.
- NEVER LEAVE FIRE UNATTENDED.

PUTTING OUT FIRE:
- BURN ALL WOOD COMPLETELY DOWN TO ASH.
- DROWN ASHES AND FILL THE PIT; THOSE ASHES THAT DON'T FIT SHOULD BE SCATTERED WITH CARE.
- REPLACE ALL SOD PIECES UNTIL PIT IS UNDETECTABLE.
- SCATTER UNUSED FIREWOOD.

EATING HIGH QUALITY, NUTRITIOUS FOODS IS AN IMPORTANT CONSIDERATION FOR THE TOURING CYCLIST WHO MAKES HIGH ENERGY DEMANDS ON HIS BODY THROUGHOUT THE DAY. CHOCOLATE BARS, SODA AND POTATO CHIPS MIGHT PROVIDE QUICK ENERGY AND NECESSARY CALORIES, BUT THIS SUGAR-HIGH IS USUALLY TEMPORARY, RESULTING IN A QUICK BURN OUT AND EXAGGERATED HUNGER PAINS SOON AFTER THIS SUGAR IS METABOLIZED.

CARBOHYDRATES, FATS AND PROTEINS MAKE UP THE FOODSTUFFS IN OUR DIET AND ARE THE BUILDING BLOCKS OF ENERGY-GIVING SUBSTANCES AND TISSUES. VITAMINS AND MINERALS FOUND IN SMALL QUANTITIES IN THE FOODS WE EAT ARE ALSO ESSENTIAL FOR GOOD HEALTH, FOR THEY REGULATE CHEMICAL REACTIONS IN OUR BODIES. REFINED AND HIGHLY PROCESSED FOODS ARE OFTEN DEFICIENT IN VITAMINS AND MINERALS.

THERE IS NO SPECIAL DIET FOR THE CYCLIST, AND SINCE THE "IDEAL" DIET IS DIFFERENT FOR EACH PERSON, THE BASIC NUTRITIONAL GOAL IS ONE OF VARIETY AND BALANCE. BY OBTAINING JUST ENOUGH PROTEIN TO MEET YOUR BODY'S NEEDS FOR MAINTENANCE AND REPAIR (PROTEIN NEEDS DO NOT INCREASE WITH EXERCISE) AND ENOUGH CALORIES FROM MOSTLY CARBOHYDRATES AND FATS TO MEET THE HIGH ENERGY NEEDS OF CYCLING (THE CYCLIST BURNS APPROXIMATELY 300-600 CALORIES IN AN HOUR) — THEN YOU HAVE PROBABLY CHOSEN YOUR IDEAL DIET.

✳·✳·✳·✳·✳·✳·✳·✳·✳·✳·✳·✳·✳·✳·✳·✳·✳·✳·✳

carbohydrates: THE MOST EFFICIENT FUEL.

CARBOHYDRATES ARE THE BODY'S MAJOR SOURCE OF ENERGY. CARBOHYDRATES ARE EASILY DIGESTED AND ARE CIRCULATED IN THE BLOOD IN THE FORM OF THE SUGAR, "GLUCOSE," WHICH IS THEN USED BY THE TISSUES FOR ENERGY. CARBOHYDRATES ARE NEEDED IN THE METABOLISM OF FAT, AND FOR ENERGY TO ASSIST PROTEINS IN THE FORMATION OF AMINO ACIDS. AN EXCESS OF CARBOHYDRATES IS STORED IN OUR BODIES AS FAT. SOME HEALTHFUL SOURCES OF CARBOHYDRATES ARE: FRUITS, PASTA, VEGETABLES, WHOLE GRAINS, LEGUMES AND SEEDS AND NUTS.

Fats: THE BODY'S STOREHOUSE. ALTHOUGH IT HAS RECEIVED A BAD REPUTATION IN OUR ERA OF FAD DIETS, FATS ARE CRUCIAL FOR STORAGE AND TRANSPORT OF FAT-SOLUBLE VITAMINS. FATS ARE ALSO DEPOSITED TO PROTECT AND

SUPPORT MANY OF THE BODY'S ORGANS. ALTHOUGH FAT DOES PLAY AN IMPORTANT ROLE IN LONG-TERM STRENUOUS ACTIVITY SUCH AS CYCLE TOURING, IT IS NOT READILY AVAILABLE FOR ENERGY; THEREFORE IT IS NOT ADVISABLE TO EAT LARGE AMOUNTS OF FAT IN ONE MEAL, BUT SPREAD YOUR FAT INTAKE THROUGHOUT THE DAY. IF YOU ARE SUFFERING FROM COLD TOES AT NIGHT IN YOUR SLEEPING BAG, TRY ADDING AN EXTRA TAB OF BUTTER TO YOUR DINNER — THE FAT IN THE BUTTER WILL NATURALLY HELP TO KEEP YOUR BODY INSULATED. FOODS SUCH AS NUTS, DAIRY PRODUCTS AND LEGUMES ARE GOOD SOURCES OF FAT THAT ALSO CONTAIN OTHER NUTRIENTS.

PEANUT BUTTER

ALL PROTEINS ARE MADE OF AMINO ACIDS WHICH ARE ESSENTIAL IN REBUILD-
ING BODY TISSUES, PROVIDE ENERGY, SERVE AS CATALYSTS FOR METABOLIC
REACTIONS AND MAKE HORMONES. UNLIKE FATS OR CARBOHYDRATES, PROTEIN
CANNOT BE STORED. EXCESS PROTEIN IS SIMPLY BROKEN DOWN FOR ENERGY
OR STORED AS FAT. BECAUSE PROTEINS DIGEST SLOWLY COMPARED TO CARBO-
HYDRATES, THEIR INTAKE SHOULD BE SPREAD THROUGHOUT THE DAY RATHER
THAN IN ONE MEAL. PROTEIN ALSO REQUIRES LARGE AMOUNTS OF WATER
TO BE BROKEN DOWN, WHICH CAN ACCELERATE DEHYDRATION IN THE CYCLIST,
WHO LOSES AN AVERAGE OF 2 CUPS AN HOUR IN PERSPIRATION.

9 OF THE 22 AMINO ACIDS ARE CONSIDERED "ESSENTIAL" IN HUMANS;
MEATS, POULTRY, FISH AND DAIRY PRODUCTS CONTAIN THE 9 ESSENTIAL
AMINO ACIDS, WHILE GRAINS, LEGUMES, SEEDS, AND NUTS LACK ONE OR
TWO OF THE ESSENTIAL AMINO ACIDS.

ALL OF THE RECIPES IN THIS BOOK (EXCEPT THOSE WITH TUNA) ARE VEGETARIAN
MEANING THAT THEIR INGREDIENTS BALANCE AMINO ACID STRENGTHS AND
WEAKNESSES OF VEGETABLE PROTEINS TO YIELD HIGH QUALITY, COMPLETE
PROTEINS. THE ADVANTAGES OF SUCH A DIET ARE NUMEROUS — A FEW
BENEFITS FOR THE CYCLIST — IT IS HIGH IN NUTRITIONAL QUALITY, EASILY
DIGESTED, LOW IN SATURATED FAT, ECONOMICAL, EASY TO PREPARE, AND
LESS WASTEFUL OF HUMAN RESOURCES (BEEF CATTLE ARE FED 14-21 LBS.
OF GRAIN TO PRODUCE ONLY ONE LB. OF BEEF).

THIS CHART ILLUSTRATES WHICH FOODS HAVE A
COMPLEMENTARY RELATIONSHIP*

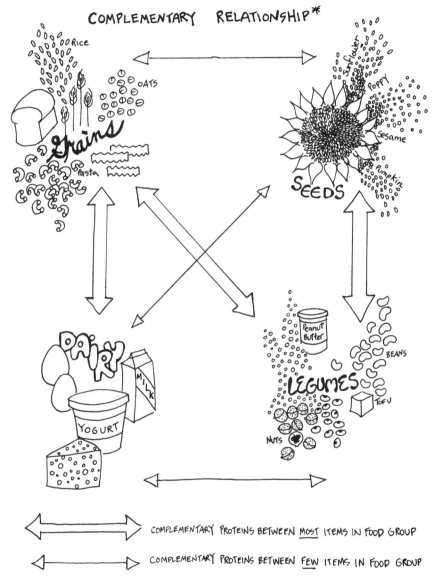

COMPLEMENTARY PROTEINS BETWEEN MOST ITEMS IN FOOD GROUP

COMPLEMENTARY PROTEINS BETWEEN FEW ITEMS IN FOOD GROUP

* FROM RECIPES FOR A SMALL PLANET BY ELLEN BUCHMAN EWALD

THE U.S. SENATE COMMITTEE ON NUTRITION AND HUMAN NEEDS HAS RECOMMENDED THE FOLLOWING DAILY CALORIC DISTRIBUTIONS FOR AMERICANS:

CARBOHYDRATES: 58%
(40-45% COMPLEX CARBOHYDRATE; 15% SUGAR)

FAT: 30%
(10% SATURATED, 20% POLY AND MONOSATURATED FAT)
PROTEIN: 12%

A Lifetime Food Cycle

THE FOLLOWING FOOD WHEEL WILL ASSIST YOU IN CHOOSING A DIET THAT WILL PROVIDE YOU WITH ENOUGH NUTRIENTS, PREVENT FATIGUE AND PROMOTE GOOD HEALTH WHILE BOTH ON AND OFF THE ROAD. IT IS BASED ON THE FOLLOWING AMERICAN DIETARY GUIDELINES ESTABLISHED BY THE U.S. DEPARTMENT OF AGRICULTURE AND THE U.S. DEPARTMENT OF FOOD SERVICES:

1. EAT A VARIETY OF FOODS FROM THE FOUR FOOD GROUPS DAILY.
2. MAINTAIN YOUR IDEAL WEIGHT.
3. AVOID TOO MUCH FAT AND CHOLESTEROL.
4. EAT FOODS WITH ADEQUATE STARCH AND FIBER.
5. AVOID TOO MUCH SUGAR.
6. AVOID TOO MUCH SODIUM.
7. IF YOU DRINK ALCOHOL, DO SO IN MODERATION.

THE FOODS IN THE INNER CIRCLE ARE DESIGNATED AS "ANYTIME" FOODS FOR THEY ARE BOTH HIGH IN NUTRITIONAL QUALITY AND DIETARY FIBER YET LOW IN SUGAR, SODIUM AND SATURATED FAT. THUS IT IS RECOMMENDED THAT THESE FOODS MAKE UP THE CORE OF YOUR DIET. WHILE THE FOODS IN THE MIDDLE RING ARE NUTRITIOUS (AND CERTAINLY TASTE GOOD!) THEY ARE RICHER THAN THOSE IN THE CENTER AND IT IS SUGGESTED THAT THEY BE EATEN "IN MODERATION." THE OUTER CIRCLE IS THE ZONE OF TEMPTATION WHICH YOU SHOULD ENTER "OCCASIONALLY" UNLESS YOU PREFER CARTING AN EXTRA INNER TUBE UP THOSE TAXING HILLS.

A RECOMMENDED FOOD CYCLE

BEANS GRAINS NUTS — 4 servings per day

OCCASIONALLY

MILK PRODUCTS — 2 servings per day

IN MODERATION

ANYTIME

BEANS GRAINS NUTS section

OCCASIONALLY: SWEET CEREALS, CROISSANTS, CAKES, BROWNIES, DOUGHNUTS

IN MODERATION: CORN BREAD, GRITS, GRANOLA, SOYBEANS, MACARONI AND CHEESE, PIZZA, PEANUT BUTTER, WHITE BREAD, WHITE RICE, NUTS, PANCAKES, AND WAFFLES WITH SYRUP

ANYTIME: DRIED BEANS, LEGUMES, WHOLE GRAINS AND BREADS, WHOLE WHEAT PASTA, TOFU, SPROUTS

MILK PRODUCTS section

OCCASIONALLY: ICE CREAM, CHEESE CAKE, FONDUE, CREAM CAKE

IN MODERATION: REGULAR COTTAGE CHEESE (4% milkfat), HARD CHEESE, SWEETENED YOGURT

ANYTIME: LOWFAT: COTTAGE CHEESE, MILK, YOGURT, SKIM CHEESES; PLAIN YOGURT, WHOLE MILK

FRUITS and VEGETABLES section — 4 servings per day

OCCASIONALLY: PICKLES, COCONUT

IN MODERATION: AVOCADO, COLE SLAW, CRANBERRY SAUCE, FRENCH FRIES, FRUIT CANNED IN SYRUP, SWEETENED FRUIT JUICE, SALTED VEGGIE JUICE

ANYTIME: MOST FRUITS AND VEGETABLES, UNSWEETENED FRUIT JUICE, UNSALTED VEGGIE JUICE, POTATOES

EGGS FISH POULTRY MEAT section — 2 servings per day

ANYTIME: TUNA (IN WATER), BAKED FISH: HADDOCK, SOLE, COD, FLOUNDER, BOILED OR BAKED CHICKEN, EGG WHITES

IN MODERATION: TUNA (OIL PACKED), SARDINES, SHRIMP, PINK SALMON, TRIMMED RED MEAT, VEAL, RUMP ROAST, PORK SHOULDER, CHICKEN OR TURKEY BAKED WITH SKIN, EGGS (3 PER WEEK)

OCCASIONALLY: SAUSAGE, LIVERWURST, FRIED CHICKEN, SPARERIBS, SALAMI, HOT DOGS, FRIED FISH, BOLOGNA, BACON

25.

A FEW WORDS ON...
WATER

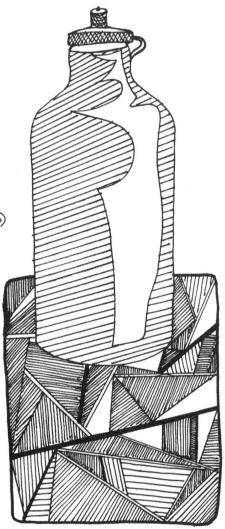

WHILE CYCLING, YOU AREN'T USUALLY AWARE THAT YOU ARE LOSING LARGE QUANTITIES OF WATER THROUGH PERSPIRATION BECAUSE IT EVAPORATES QUICKLY. HOWEVER, THE AVERAGE CYCLIST NEEDS WELL OVER TWO QUARTS A DAY (3 OZ. FOR EVERY 100 CALORIES OF FOOD CONSUMED) OUR BODIES USE WATER FOR MOST OF ITS FUNCTIONS: DIGESTING FOOD, CARRYING NUTRIENTS TO CELLS, LUBRICATING MOVING PARTS SUCH AS JOINTS, PUMPING OF THE HEART AND FLUSHING AWAY CHEMICAL WASTES SUCH AS UREA, WHICH IS PRODUCED DURING PROTEIN METABOLISM. SYMPTOMS OF DEHYDRATION ARE HEADACHES AND FATIGUE, AND ARE SIGNALS THAT YOUR BODY NEEDS WATER. YOU CAN PREVENT DEHYDRATION BY SIMPLY DRINKING GENEROUSLY THROUGHOUT THE DAY. RATHER THAN RISK CRAMPS FROM GUZZLING DOWN AN ENTIRE WATER BOTTLE IN 30 SECONDS, IT IS BEST TO DRINK SMALL SIPS EVERY FEW MILES.

MANY FOODS SUCH AS FRUITS AND VEGETABLES HAVE LARGE PERCENTAGES OF WATER AND ARE GOOD THIRST QUENCHERS.

A FINAL NOTE: DON'T RISK DIARRHEA OR A STOMACH BUG FROM DRINKING CONTAMINATED WATER.— KNOW YOUR WATER SOURCE — IF YOU'RE NOT SURE THAT ITS CLEAN, DON'T DRINK IT UNLESS ABSOLUTELY NECESSARY. PURIFY ANY WATER YOU ARE SKEPTICAL OF BY BOILING FOR 10 MINUTES, OR BY ADDING WATER PURIFICATION TABLETS.

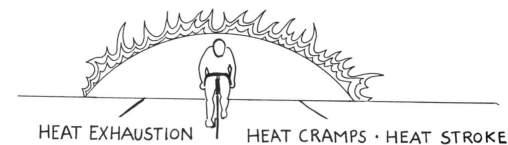

HEAT EXHAUSTION · HEAT CRAMPS · HEAT STROKE

WHENEVER YOU EXERT YOURSELF PHYSICALLY, YOU SHOULD BE AWARE OF THE SYMPTOMS OF HEAT STROKE, HEAT CRAMPS AND HEAT EXHAUSTION. ALTHOUGH THEIR SYMPTOMS AND TREATMENT ARE DIFFERENT, THEY ARE ALL A RESULT OF YOUR BODY'S INABILITY TO REGULATE EXCESSIVE HEAT. EACH CONDITION SHOULD BE TAKEN SERIOUSLY AND TREATED IMMEDIATELY.

HEAT EXHAUSTION

SYMPTOMS: PALE FACE, PROFUSE PERSPIRATION, CLAMMY SKIN, WEAK PULSE, SHALLOW BREATHING, LETHARGIC. NAUSEA, VOMITING, DIZZINESS AND UNSTEADINESS ARE USUALLY PRESENT.

TREATMENT: HAVE PERSON LIE DOWN, WITH THEIR HEAD AT THE SAME LEVEL AS THE REST OF THE BODY, IN A WELL VENTILATED PLACE.

COVER THE PERSON LIGHTLY AND ADMINISTER ½ t. SALT MIXED IN A GLASS OF WATER. WARM COFFEE OR TEA CAN BE DRUNK, BUT CALL A DOCTOR AND DISCUSS ANY FURTHER TREATMENT.

HEAT CRAMPS:

PAINFUL CRAMPS IN MUSCLES OF LEGS, ARMS OR ABDOMEN MIGHT ACCOMPANY SYMPTOMS OF HEAT EXHAUSTION. PUTTING FIRM PRESSURE ON AFFECTED AREA MAY BRING RELIEF.

HEAT STROKE:

SYMPTOMS: FLUSHED RED FACE, HOT DRY SKIN, RAPID PULSE (OPPOSITE FROM HEAT EXHAUSTION) HIGH BODY TEMPERATURE (107°+). THE PERSON FEELS DIZZY AND HAS A HEADACHE, DRY MOUTH AND SKIN. UNCONSCIOUSNESS CAN FOLLOW AND ABOUT ¼ ALL SERIOUS CASES ARE FATAL.

TREATMENT: PLACE PERSON ON BACK, WITH HEAD ELEVATED, IN A COOL PLACE; REMOVE CLOTHES AND APPLY WET CLOTHES OR ICE BAGS. COOL BODY WITH SMALL AMOUNTS OF COLD WATER. DO NOT GIVE STIMULANTS (COFFEE, TEA, SODA). A DOCTOR SHOULD BE CALLED IMMEDIATELY.

HYPO THERMIA

OFTENTIMES WHEN YOU ARE TOURING IN THE SPRING OR AUTUMN, THERE WILL BE DAYS WHEN THE WEATHER TAKES AN ABRUPT SHIFT FROM SUNNY AND WARM IN THE MORNING, TO RAINY AND FRIGID IN THE AFTERNOON. ANXIOUS TO GET TO CAMP, YOU MIGHT TRY TO BRAVE THE BITING COLD AND PUSH HARD FOR THOSE EXTRA MILES, BUT INSTEAD YOU FIND YOURSELF SHIVERING AND HAVING DIFFICULTY PEDALING.

THE ABOVE SYMPTOMS SHOULD BE TAKEN SERIOUSLY, FOR THEY INDICATE THE ONSET OF HYPOTHERMIA — A CONDITION IN WHICH YOUR BODY IS LOSING HEAT FASTER THAN IT CAN PRODUCE IT AND IS UNABLE TO MAINTAIN A NORMAL 98° BODY TEMPERATURE. YOU SHOULD ALWAYS BE AWARE THAT WHILE THE AIR TEMPERATURE MAY BE 40°, COMBINED WITH WIND AND THE SPEED OF YOU AND YOUR BICYCLE IT MAY DROP TO BELOW 15°.

DRESSING AND EATING PROPERLY ARE THE KEYS IN PREVENTING HYPOTHERMIA. EATING PLENTY OF HIGH ENERGY AND EASILY DIGESTIBLE FOODS LIKE GORP, COOKIES AND FRUIT IS CRUCIAL WHEN RIDING IN THE COLD. THESE FOODS WILL NOT ONLY GIVE YOU AN EXTRA ENERGY BOOST, BUT THEY WILL HELP YOUR BODY MAINTAIN A CONSTANT TEMPERATURE — OR, PUT MORE SIMPLY:

NO FOOD → NO FUEL → COLD ENGINE!!

WHEN IT IS COLD YOU MAY NOT FEEL LIKE DRINKING, BUT THE MORE DEHYDRATED YOU BECOME, THE LESS EFFICIENT YOU ARE IN CIRCULATING HEAT. TRY TO TAKE ADVANTAGE OF ROADSIDE DINERS OR GAS STATIONS TO WARM YOURSELF UP AND DRINK DOWN SOME NEEDED FLUIDS.

Symptoms:

1. SHIVERING, DECREASED MUSCLE COORDINATION, AS BODY CHILLS FURTHER, SPEECH BECOMES SLUGGISH.
2. POOR JUDGEMENT, SLUGGISH THINKING (HYPOTHERMIA VICTIMS ARE USUALLY THE LAST ONES TO REALIZE THEY HAVE HYPOTHERMIA)
3. UNCONTROLLABLE AND JERKY MOVEMENTS, IRRATIONAL BEHAVIOR. VICTIM'S BODY TEMPERATURE IS BELOW 95°
4. COMPLETE UNCOORDINATION AND POTENTIAL UNCONSCIOUSNESS. SLUGGISH MUSCLES, NO REFLEXES AND FAINT BREATHING, ERRATIC HEARTBEAT AND EVENTUAL DEATH.

Treatment:

1. GET INTO WARM AND DRY CLOTHES.
2. STOP AND WARM UP IN HEATED SHELTER. HAVE A HOT DRINK, BUT DEFINITELY AVOID ALCOHOLIC BEVERAGES.
3. IF NO HEATED SHELTER IS AVAILABLE— FIND AN OUTSIDE SHELTER (GROUP OF TREES) FROM WIND AND RAIN AND HAVE VICTIM CHANGE INTO DRY CLOTHES AND WRAP HIM IN A SLEEPING BAG. ADMINISTER HOT DRINKS.
4. IF VICTIM IS IN STAGE ④, TRANSPORT HIM TO A HOSPITAL <u>IMMEDIATELY</u>.

The Warming Hut

The Recipes

- IF YOU USE DRIED BEANS LET THEM SOAK FOR AT LEAST 2 HOURS AND ALLOW TO COOK UNTIL TENDER (1-2 HOURS—SEE APPENDIX)
- LEARN THE MANNERISMS OF YOUR STOVE SO YOU CAN CONTROL HEAT PROPERLY.
- DON'T OVERCOOK FOODS BY COOKING AT A HIGH HEAT OR TOO LONG.
- START STEWS, ETC. WITH ENOUGH WATER; WATER WILL ALSO HELP COOK VEGETABLES BY STEAMING THEM.
- STIR THICKENED FOODS OFTEN.
- DON'T OVERSALT OR OVERSPICE.
- MARGARINE KEEPS BETTER THAN BUTTER.
- SAVE VEGETABLE COOKING WATER FOR SAUCES AND STOCK.
- PUT A FEW PINCHES OF RICE IN A SALT CONTAINER TO KEEP IT FROM CLUMPING.
- KEEP COOKBOOKS AND RECIPES IN A PLASTIC BAG.
- DON'T STIR MORE THAN YOU HAVE TO WHILE COOKING, THE EXTRA OXYGEN YOU INCORPORATE WILL BREAK DOWN SOME FOOD ELEMENTS AND EFFECT NUTRIENTS.
- TO PREVENT LUMPING OF FLOUR OR POWDERED MILK, ALWAYS DISSOLVE THEM IN A BIT OF COLD WATER
- HONEY CAN BE USED TO REPLACE SUGAR (BUT CUT AMOUNT IN HALF).
- ALUMINUM FOIL HAS MANY USEFUL PURPOSES: WRAPPING CORN ON THE COB, COVERING POTS WHILE COOKING, COOKING FOOD AND AS AN EXTRA PLATE.
- IF YOU WANT TO KEEP FOODS FAIRLY COLD, PACK THEM IN THE BOTTOM OF YOUR PACK OR WRAP THEM IN A TOWEL OR SLEEPING BAG OR PAD.
- KEEP FUEL BOTTLES AWAY FROM FOOD IN YOUR PACK.
- TRY MAKING SALAD IN A PLASTIC BAG IF YOUR OUT OF POTS.
- RUB BOTTOMS OF POT WITH SOAP TO PREVENT THEM FROM BECOMING COVERED WITH SOOT
- TO THICKEN FOODS ADD: 1 PART FLOUR : 1 PART WATER, POTATOES, CREAM OF WHEAT, AND WHEAT GERM.
- **IN CASE OF FOOD SHORTAGE, LEADER CAN BE EATEN**

GOOD MORNING!

BREAKFAST

WAKING UP TO THE CRISP, STILL AIR OF THE MORNING AND THINKING ABOUT THE ADVENTURES THE DAY HOLDS IS CONDUCIVE TO AN APPETITE. IN THE MORNING, AFTER YOUR BODY HAS LONG DIGESTED DINNER, IT ONLY MAKES SENSE TO REFUEL YOUR BODY WELL. SO, BEFORE YOU EMBARK ON A PHYSICALLY DEMANDING DAY, FEAST ON A BREAKFAST THAT WILL GET YOU OVER THE HILLS TILL LUNCH. LIKE OTHER CAMPING MEALS, BREAKFAST CAN BE ECLECTIC; I KNOW OF BACKPACKERS WHO SWEAR BY LEFTOVER DINNER—BEANS AND RICE FOR BREAKFAST. BUT IF YOUR PALATE IS USED TO MORE CONVENTIONAL TASTES, THERE ARE UNLIMITED VARIETIES OF PANCAKES, CEREALS, EGGS AND OF COURSE OATMEAL.

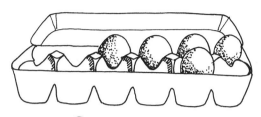

EGGS

SCRAMBLED EGGS ARE THE EASIEST WAY TO PREPARE EGGS FOR LARGE GROUPS OF PEOPLE. YOU CAN SATISFY DIFFERENT TASTES AS YOU GO ALONG. I CALL IT —

EGG A LA ANYTHING

1 DOZEN EGGS   serves approximately 6
1/2 – 1 C. MILK
DASH SALT

BEAT: EGGS AND MILK
POUR: MIXTURE INTO OILED FRY PAN.
SCRAMBLE: WITH ONE OR MORE OF THE FOLLOWING INGREDIENTS:

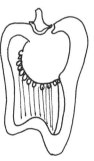

* SAUTEED ONIONS, APPLE SLICES, BLACK PEPPER AND CINNAMON
* SAUTEED MUSHROOMS, PEPPER, TOMATOES, OREGANO, SPRINKLE CHEDDAR CHEESE ON TOP BEFORE SERVING

* SAUTEED ZUCCHINI, PEPPERS, FRESH DILL, PARSLEY AND SWISS CHEESE
* SAUTEED TOMATOES WITH GARLIC, WALNUTS, SLICED POTATO
* SAUTEED MUNG BEAN SPROUTS, CHOPPED ONION, RAISINS AND BASIL
* SAUTEED BROCCOLI, SCALLIONS, CREAM CHEESE, CARAWAY SEEDS.

Citrus Surprise

YOU WILL NEED HOT COALS FROM A CAMPFIRE. FOR EACH PERSON OBTAIN: 1 JUICY ORANGE, AN EGG, MUFFIN BATTER (STORE BOUGHT) AND TIN FOIL.

CUT AN ORANGE IN HALF CROSSWISE AND SCOOP OUT THE FRUIT OF BOTH HALVES. EAT THE FRUIT AT YOUR LEISURE.

BREAK EGG INTO ONE HALF OF ORANGE SHELL. POUR BATTER FOR ONE MUFFIN INTO OTHER HALF. WRAP EACH HALF IN A PIECE OF FOIL AND TWIST TOP.

PLACE FOIL WRAPPED ORANGE HALVES IN HOT COALS FOR 15 MINUTES.

EGGS IN A NEST

for 6

6 SLICES BREAD
6 EGGS
6 SLICES CHEESE

CUT: SMALL CIRCLE INTO EACH SLICE OF BREAD.
FRY: BREAD IN BUTTER.
BREAK: ONE EGG INTO EACH HOLE IN BREAD.
POACH: EGG UNTIL COOKED, THEN PLACE SLICE OF CHEESE ON TOP AND ALLOW TO MELT.

Banana Frittata

serves 3

6 EGGS
3 BANANAS ~ RIPE
1/2 C. RAISINS
1 t. NUTMEG AND CINNAMON
1/2 C. YOGURT

SAUTÉ: BANANAS IN BUTTER
ADD: BEATEN EGGS, RAISINS AND SPICES
COOK: 5 MINUTES ON LOW HEAT
SERVE: TOPPED WITH YOGURT

Scrambled Tuna

serves 3

6 EGGS (MIXED WELL)
1 CAN TUNA (WATER-PACKED)
2 TOMATOES, CHOPPED
1 C. GRATED CHEESE
1/2 C. WHEAT GERM
OREGANO, DILL WEED TO TASTE

SAUTÉ: TOMATO AND TUNA IN OIL
ADD: EGG MIXTURE AND ALLOW TO SIMMER 1 MINUTE
ADD: GRATED CHEESE (SWISS IS GREAT) AND WHEAT GERM AND STIR.
SERVE: ON TOAST OR BAGELS

EGGS! MORE! EGGS!

EGGS ARE A GREAT FOOD FOR THE CYCLE TOURIST ANY TIME OF DAY, FOR THEY ARE HIGH IN NUTRITION, VERSATILE, INEXPENSIVE AND JUST TASTE **GOOD**! WHEN YOU'RE RIDING IN FARMCOUNTRY KEEP YOUR EYES OUT FOR FRESH AND DELICIOUS FARM EGGS. TRY THE FOLLOWING DIFFERENT VERSIONS OF POACHED EGGS FOR A QUICK GOURMET BREAKFAST OR DINNER.

Poached Egg Stew (serves 3)

1 C. TOMATO SAUCE
2 TOMATOES, DICED
2 GREEN PEPPERS, CHOPPED
2 ONIONS, DICED
OREGANO, BASIL, TO TASTE
6 EGGS
1/2 C. PARMESAN OR OTHER GRATED CHEESE.

SAUTÉ: ONIONS AND PEPPER IN HOT, OILED FRY PAN, COOK UNTIL TENDER
ADD: TOMATOES AND SIMMER UNTIL TOMATOES ARE COOKED.
ADD: SAUCE AND SEASONINGS
POACH: EGGS IN VEGETABLE MIXTURE AND TOP WITH GRATED CHEESE
SERVE: ON TOAST OR WITH A PITA BREAD.

Huevos Rancheros (serves 3)

1 GREEN PEPPER, CHOPPED
1 ONION, DICED
2 C. COOKED RICE (GOOD USE FOR LEFTOVER DINNER RICE)
2 TOMATOES, DICED.
BASIL, OREGANO TO TASTE.
6 EGGS

SAUTÉ: VEGGIES IN OIL UNTIL TENDER.
ADD: COOKED RICE AND MIX.
MAKE: 6 INDENTATIONS IN RICE AND CRACK ONE EGG INTO EACH INDENTATION.
COOK: AND SIMMER 5-10 MINUTES UNTIL EGGS ARE DONE.

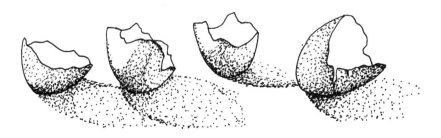

Green Eggs & Mushrooms

serves 3

1 PACKAGE SPINACH
1 ONION DICED FINE
1/2 lb. MUSHROOMS SLICED
1 C. RICOTTA OR COTTAGE CHEESE
6 EGGS
3 BAGELS OR SLICES WHOLE WHEAT BREAD.

SAUTÉ: ONIONS AND MUSHROOMS IN OIL UNTIL TENDER.
ADD: BROKEN UP PIECES OF SPINACH AND ADD A LITTLE WATER TO STEAM.
ADD: CHEESE AND STIR GENTLY

MAKE: 6 INDENTATIONS IN SPINACH MIXTURE AND CRACK AN EGG INTO EACH.
SIMMER: UNTIL EGGS ARE COOKED TO YOUR PREFERENCE.
SERVE: ON TOAST OR BAGELS.

Hash Browns

serves 3-6

3 C. <u>FINELY</u> DICED RAW POTATOES
1 SMALL ONION, DICED.
1 T. PARSLEY
1/2 t. SALT
1/4 t. BLACK PEPPER

MIX: ALL INGREDIENTS AND SPREAD INTO HOT, OILED FRY PAN.
PRESS: POTATO MIXTURE WITH SPATULA INTO A FLAT CAKE.
COOK: POTATO MIXTURE SLOWLY AND SHAKE IT TO KEEP IT FROM STICKING.
FLIP: POTATO MIXTURE WHEN BROWNED AND ALLOW TO SIMMER 5 MINUTES.
TOP: WITH BUTTER. AND SERVE WITH EGGS

PANCAKES

COOKING PANCAKES IS TRICKY BUSINESS ON THE UNEVEN HEAT OF A CAMP STOVE; USUALLY THE FIRST FEW ATTEMPTS RESULT IN A BATCH OF DISASTROUS, HALF-COOKED AMOEBA-LIKE EXCUSES FOR PANCAKES. BUT WITH PRACTICE IN THE ART OF FRYING AND FLIPPING, AND SOME ORGANIZATION BETWEEN COOKS, YOU'LL SOON HAVE BATCHES OF PATTIES DISAPPEAR BEFORE YOUR EYES!

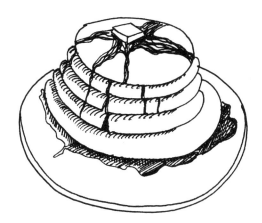

THE BASIC BATTER:

Serves 6

2 C. WHOLE WHEAT FLOUR
3 T. BAKING POWDER
1 t. SALT
2 EGGS
2 C. MILK OR YOGURT
4 T. OIL
SEASONINGS: CINNAMON, NUTMEG
1 T. HONEY

FOR MORE EXCITING PATTIES ADD 1 C.
OF ANY OF THE FOLLOWING TO BATTER:
  WHEAT GERM, RAISINS, OAT FLAKES,
  CORN MEAL, SESAME SEEDS, CHOPPED
  APPLES, SLICED BANANAS, NUTS,
  BLUEBERRIES, COTTAGE CHEESE....
  (TO NAME A FEW)

MIX: DRY INGREDIENTS WITH CHOICE
  INGREDIENTS.
ADD: MILK, HONEY, EGGS AND OIL
STIR: UNTIL MOIST (IF TOO MUCH LIQUID,
  ADD MORE FLOUR)
FRY: BY SPOONFUL OF MIXTURE ONTO
  HOT, WELL OILED FRY PAN. WHEN
  TOP OF PATTIES BUBBLE, FLIP
  AND COOK UNTIL DONE. DO NOT
  PRESS PATTIES WITH SPATULA.

FRENCH TOAST

serves 6-8

FRENCH TOAST IS EASIER TO PREPARE AND MASTER THAN PANCAKES, YET THE EGG AND THE MILK BATTER TRANSFORM ORDINARY BREAD INTO A RICH TASTING MEAL. HERE'S A CHEESY ADAPTION THAT INCREASES THE FLAVOR AND THE AMOUNT OF PROTEIN.

1 DOZEN EGGS
1 LB. COTTAGE CHEESE (OR 1 C. MILK)
1 LOAF WHOLE WHEAT BREAD
PEPPER, SALT, NUTMEG AND BROWN SUGAR TO TASTE.

MIX: EGGS, CHEESE AND SPICES IN A POT
SOAK: BREAD IN MIXTURE
FRY: PIECES INDIVIDUALLY UNTIL BROWNED
SERVE: WITH SYRUP OR TOPPING

UN-NUTTY FRENCH TOAST

IF AFTER ALL THESE YEARS YOU HAVE BEEN UNDER THE IMPRESSION THAT THE PEANUT WAS ACTUALLY A NUT, THEN I'M AFRAID I'LL HAVE TO EXPOSE THE HARD FACTS. THE PEANUT IS A MEMBER OF THE LEGUME FAMILY AND GROWS ON A LOW, BUSHLIKE PLANT IN TROPICAL REGIONS. BUT DON'T LET ITS MISTAKEN IDENTITY PREVENT YOU FROM ENJOYING THIS UNNUTTY TREAT

1/2 C. PEANUT BUTTER
8 SLICES WHOLE GRAIN BREAD
2 EGGS
1/2 C. MILK
1/4 t. BUTTER

MAKE: 4 PEANUT BUTTER SANDWICHES
MIX: EGGS, MILK
DIP: SANDWICHES IN EGG/MILK MIXTURE
FRY: SANDWICHES IN BUTTER OR MARGARINE.

38.

POTATO PANCAKES

POTATO PANCAKES ARE A HEFTY MEAL FOR FUELING YOUR ENGINE BEFORE YOU BEGIN A LONG DAY OF TOURING (AND THEY ARE GUARANTEED TO GET YOU AT LEAST 10 MILES PER PANCAKE), THEY ARE ALSO GREAT FOR SILENCING GROWLING BELLIES WHEN DINNERTIME ROLLS AROUND.

6 LARGE POTATOES
3 EGGS, BEATEN
1T. WHEAT GERM
1T. WHOLE WHEAT FLOUR
1 SMALL ONION, DICED FINE
DASH SALT, SOY SAUCE.
OIL FOR FRYING
APPLESAUCE, YOGURT OR COTTAGE CHEESE FOR TOPPING.

GRATE: POTATOES
SQUEEZE: OUT WATER FROM POTATOES WITH PAPER TOWEL OR CLEAN CLOTH.
MIX: POTATOES, WHEAT GERM, WHOLE WHEAT FLOUR, ONIONS, SOY SAUCE, SALT, AND EGGS
FRY: BY SPOONFULS ONTO HOT, WELL-OILED FRY PAN.
TOP: WITH APPLESAUCE, COTTAGE CHEESE OR YOGURT.

FRUITY TOPPINGS

MAPLE SYRUP IS NOT THE ONLY TOPPING THAT TASTES GOOD DRIBBLED ALL OVER YOUR PANCAKES OR FRENCH TOAST ~ TRY SOAKING THEM UP WITH ANY OF THE FOLLOWING FRUITY SAUCES.

- YOGURT APPLESAUCE: YOGURT MIXED WITH HONEY AND APPLESAUCE.

- HONEY-COCONUT — COMBINE 3/4 C. HONEY, 2 T. MELTED BUTTER, 3/4 C. GRATED COCONUT.

- MOLASSES AND ORANGE SAUCE: 1/2 C. MOLASSES, 1/4 C. BROWN SUGAR, 1/3 C ORANGE JUICE, 1/4 C. BUTTER, 1 T. GRATED ORANGE RIND. COMBINE INGREDIENTS AND HEAT UNTIL BLENDED.

- BLUE CHEESE SAUCE: COMBINE AND HEAT— 1 C. BLUEBERRIES, 1/2 C. YOGURT, 1/2 C. COTTAGE CHEESE, AND 1/4 C. MAPLE SYRUP

- FRUITED HONEY SAUCE: 3 PEARS OR APPLES CORED AND DICED, 1/2 C. HONEY 1 T. LEMON JUICE, 1/4 C. RAISINS. COMBINE INGREDIENTS AND COOK SLOWLY UNTIL FRUIT IS TENDER

- APPLE-NUT SAUCE: COMBINE 1 C. APPLESAUCE, 1/2 C. WALNUTS, 3 t. CINNAMON AND 1T. BUTTER.

- CREAMY STRAWBERRY SAUCE: COMBINE AND HEAT: 1 C. YOGURT, 1 lb DICED STRAWBERRIES, 1 T HONEY AND 3 t. NUTMEG

⑨//⑨//⑨//⑨ WHOLE GRAINS ⑨//⑨//⑨//⑨//

WHOLE GRAINS ARE A FILLING ACCOMPANIMENT TO EGGS, OR CAN BE SERVED ALONE TOPPED WITH YOGURT OR MILK FOR A COMPLETE AND SATISFYING MEAL. GRAINS SUCH AS CRACKED WHEAT, CRACKED BULGUR, KASHA, OATS, COUS COUS OR MILLET CAN BE PREPARED IN LESS THAN A HALF AN HOUR. TRY COMBINING DIFFERENT GRAINS AND SEASONING THEM WITH SALT, CINNAMON, NUTMEG, SOY SAUCE OR CARAWAY. ADD HONEY, MAPLE SYRUP, OR DRIED FRUIT TO SWEETEN.

THREE BEAR MUSH

(serves 4-5 Hungry Bears)

1 C. CRACKED BULGUR OR CRACKED WHEAT
1 C. QUICK OATS
1/4 C. WHEAT GERM
1/4 C. SOY GRITS
1/4 C. SESAME SEEDS
1/4 C. COCONUT
1/2 C. DRIED FRUIT
4-5 C. BOILING WATER

BOIL: WATER
ADD: INGREDIENTS SLOWLY AND SIMMER UNTIL GRAINS ARE COOKED (ADD MORE WATER IF NECESSARY)

Mighty oats

serves 4-5

2 C. QUICK OATS
1 C. RAISINS
3 APPLES, DICED FINE
2 C. APPLESAUCE
2 C. YOGURT
1/2 C. SUNFLOWER SEEDS
1/2 C. WHEAT GERM
CINNAMON, NUTMEG TO TASTE
4 C. BOILING WATER

ADD: OATS TO BOILING WATER
SIMMER AND ADD: APPLES, RAISINS SUNFLOWER SEEDS AND SPICES.
COOK: 3 MINUTES AND ADD WHEAT GERM AND MORE WATER IF NECESSARY.
SERVE: TOPPED WITH YOGURT AND APPLESAUCE.

OATMEAL
THE INCREDIBLE EDIBLE MUSH

YUM!

QUICK QUAKER OATS

OATMEAL HAS RECEIVED A BAD REPUTATION AS BEING TASTELESS GOO, BUT IT IS QUICK, EASY, AND AS EXCITING AS YOUR PALATE PRESCRIBES.

4 C. OATS : 4 C. WATER
DASH SALT

BOIL: WATER
ADD: OATS AND SIMMER FOR
    ONE MINUTE
NOW FOR THE <u>REAL MEAL</u>;
WHILE IT'S COOKING
ADD: A HEAPING OF:
- BANANAS, RAISINS, NUTMEG
- CHOPPED APPLES, CHOPPED WALNUTS, RAISINS AND CINNAMON
- GRAPENUTS, PINEAPPLE, DATES
- BLUEBERRIES, SUNFLOWER SEEDS
- GRANOLA, DICED PEARS, CLOVES
- WHEAT GERM, SLICED PEACHES
- SUBSTITUTE 1/2 OATMEAL FOR WHEATENA

COOK: ADDITIONAL 3 MINUTES AND ADD MORE WATER IF NECESSARY
BEFORE SERVING TOP WITH:
- COTTAGE CHEESE
- YOGURT
- MILK
- HONEY, MAPLE SYRUP, BROWN SUGAR, MOLASSES, OR BUTTER.

41.

KASHA AND COUS COUS

KASHA IS THE SEED FROM THE GRASSLIKE HERB BUCKWHEAT. IT IS A STAPLE IN RUSSIA AND BRITTANY AND IS A HEARTY MEAL WHEN SERVED AT BREAKFAST WITH FRUIT OR AT DINNER AS A RICE SUBSTITUTE.

BREAKFAST KASHA (serves 6)

1 C. KASHA (BUCKWHEAT GROATS)
1 EGG LIGHTLY BEATEN
2 BANANAS SLICED
1 C. RAISINS
2 1/2 C. BOILING WATER

MIX: DRY KASHA WITH EGG AND HEAT MIXTURE OVER MEDIUM HEAT
ADD: REMAINING INGREDIENTS AND BRING TO BOIL
COVER: AND SIMMER: 20 MINUTES UNTIL GRAIN IS COOKED.

COUSCOUS IS A STAPLE OF NORTH AFRICAN CUISINE. IT HAS A DELICATE FLAVOR WITH A TEXTURE SIMILAR TO CORN GRITS. IT IS SIMPLE TO PREPARE AND CAN BE DELICIOUSLY MADE WITH FRUIT FOR BREAKFAST OR AS A RICE SUBSTITUTE FOR DINNER.

BREAKFAST COUS COUS (for 4)

1 C. COUS COUS
2 C. BOILING WATER
2 T. BUTTER OR MARGARINE

BOIL: WATER
ADD: COUS COUS AND BUTTER AND SIMMER, WHILE STIRRING, THREE MINUTES
ADD: ANY OF THE FOLLOWING:
- 2 BANANAS DICED, WALNUTS
- RAISINS, DRIED PINEAPPLE
- 1 C. COTTAGE CHEESE
- DICED APPLES, SUNFLOWER SEEDS.
SIMMER: UNTIL COOKED

HOMINY GRITS
(serves 4)

1 C. HOMINY GRITS
3 C. MILK
1 t. SALT
2 EGGS
6 T. BUTTER
1 C. GRATED CHEESE.

STIR: GRITS INTO MILK, ADD SALT AND COOK OVER MEDIUM HEAT, STIRRING OFTEN SO MIXTURE DOES NOT BURN. WHEN MIXTURE IS THICK, REMOVE FROM HEAT AND...
ADD: EGGS AND 1 C. WATER, STIR VIGOROUSLY.
RETURN TO HEAT: AND COOK UNTIL THICKENED.
ADD: BUTTER AND CHEESE AND
SIMMER: 5 MINUTES

SINCE THE DAWN OF THE "NATURAL FOOD" CRAZE, THE POPULARITY OF GRANOLA HAS SKYROCKETED. WHILE YOU CAN BUY "ALL NATURAL GRANOLA" AT THE SUPERMARKET, IT IS USUALLY VERY EXPENSIVE AND LOADED WITH SUGAR. BY MAKING IT AT HOME (IN LESS THAN AN HOUR) YOU CAN SAVE MONEY AND VARY THE INGREDIENTS TO SUIT YOUR TASTE BUDS.

BASICALLY GRANOLA IS A HIGH PROTEIN CEREAL MIXTURE OF **GRAINS** (RYE FLAKES, WHEAT FLAKES, OATS) **NUTS, SEEDS, DRIED FRUIT,** OIL AND A **SWEETENER** THAT, WHEN EATEN WITH MILK, CAN SUPPLY UP TO 35% OF YOUR DAILY PROTEIN NEEDS.

THE FOLLOWING VERSION OF GRANOLA IS MADE WITH MOLASSES WHICH NOT ONLY GIVES IT A RICH FLAVOR, BUT ALSO PROVIDES AN EXCELLENT SOURCE OF IRON.

Betty's Molasses Crunch

3 C. ROLLED OATS	1/3 C. COCONUT	1/3 C. OIL
1/2 C. WHEAT FLAKES	1/4 C. SESAME SEEDS	3/4 C. MOLASSES } MIX
1/2 C. RYE FLAKES	1/2 t. CINNAMON	1/2 t. VANILLA
1/2 C. SOY FLAKES	1/4 t. CLOVES	
1/2 C. WHEAT GERM	1/4 t. GINGER	
1/2 C. PEANUTS	1/2 t. SALT	
3/4 C. RAISINS		

SPREAD AND MIX: ALL INGREDIENTS ON COOKIE SHEET.
BAKE: 15 MINUTES AT 275°.
TURN AND MIX: BAKE ADDITIONAL 15 MINUTES.

OPTIONAL SUBSTITUTIONS:
1/2 C. PEANUTS: 1/2 CUP SUNFLOWER SEEDS, 1/2 C. SOY NUTS, 1/2 C. WALNUTS
3/4 C. RAISINS: 3/4 C. DRIED APPLE, 3/4 C. DATES,
1/2 C. RYE FLAKES: 1 C. WHEAT GERM, 1 C. BRAN FLAKES
3/4 C. MOLASSES: 3/4 C. HONEY, 3/4 C. MAPLE SUGAR

BREAKFAST on the ROAD

OFTEN WHEN I FEEL LIKE HITTING THE ROAD EARLY AND DON'T WANT TO BOTHER WITH COOKING BREAKFAST, I'LL RIDE A FEW MILES UNTIL I DISCOVER A GROCERY STORE WHERE I CAN PURCHASE A VARIETY OF COLD TREATS SUCH AS: FRUIT, CEREAL, OR NUTS TOPPED WITH YOGURT, MILK OR COTTAGE CHEESE. ALTHOUGH IN THE EARLY MORNING MY GROWLING STOMACH IS AT THE MERCY OF THE COUNTRY GROCER'S OFTEN LIMITED SUPPLY, I TRY TO BE INVENTIVE WITH THE FOOD AT HAND. OCCASIONALLY, HOWEVER, I AM PLEASANTLY SURPRISED TO FIND FRESH MUFFINS OR HOT COFFEE AT THE CHECK-OUT COUNTER TO ADD SOME WARMTH TO MY SIMPLE BREAKFAST AFFAIR.

Fruity

GRAPES ✱ BANANAS ✱ RAISINS
MELONS ✱ APPLES ✱ ORANGES ✱
BANANAS ✱ STRAWBERRIES ✱
PINEAPPLES ✱ BLUEBERRIES ✱
GRAPEFRUIT ✱ PEARS ✱ PEACHES

MIX TOGETHER:
COTTAGE CHEESE
YOGURT
MILK

Crunchy

GRAPENUTS ✱ HONEY
SHREDDED WHEAT ✱ CINNAMON
WHEAT GERM ✱ WALNUTS
PEANUTS ✱ SUNFLOWER SEEDS
CASHEWS ✱ SESAME SEEDS

Creamy

MILK MILK PLAIN YOGURT COTTAGE CHEESE

44.

IN ADDITION TO YOUR THREE NORMAL MEALS A DAY, OCCASIONAL NIBBLING ON SNACKS SUCH AS FRUIT, NUTS, GRANOLA OR VEGETABLE STICKS, HELP KEEP YOUR ENERGY HIGH ALL DAY LONG. DON'T WAIT UNTIL YOU'RE "STARVING" TO EAT— IN THE MORNING AT BREAKFAST, PACK A SMALL BAG OF SNACKS AND CARRY IT IN A CONVENIENT PLACE WHERE YOU CAN REACH AS YOU RIDE.

WHEN YOU DO DECIDE TO SIT TOGETHER FOR THAT MID—DAY BREAK, THE MEAL SHOULD BE SIMPLE, YET SATISFYING. PLAN YOUR ROUTE SO YOU INTERSECT A LIKELY PLACE TO BUY FOOD FOR LUNCH. AVOID THE TEMPTATION TO FILL UP ON ICE CREAM, SODA OR CANDY INSTEAD OF A BALANCED MEAL. SOME WHOLESOME, FILLING IDEAS FOR LUNCH: FRUIT, CHEESE, YOGURT, VEGETABLE STICKS (I AM A FAN OF CARROTS) DIPPED IN PEANUT BUTTER, CRACKERS, NUTS, DRIED FRUIT AND THERE ARE OF COURSE INFINITE SANDWICH CREATIONS. TO NAME A FEW OF MY FAVORITE SANDWICH SPREADS:

PEANUT BUTTER CO-STARRING ONE OR MORE OF THE FOLLOWING: BANANA, RAISINS, HONEY, CHOPPED APPLE, SPROUTS, CHOPPED CELERY, CARROTS, CHEESE AND OF COURSE JAM.

COTTAGE CHEESE OR **CREAM CHEESE** MIXED WITH: CHOPPED CARROT AND CELERY; RAISIN AND PINEAPPLE; CHOPPED ONIONS, SLICED TOMATO AND CUCUMBER, DICED APPLE, WALNUT AND CINNAMON

TUNA FISH SALAD — A CAN OF TUNA MIXED WITH: (serves 3)
- 1/2 C COTTAGE CHEESE
- SHREDDED CARROT
- 1/4 C. MAYONNAISE OR YOGURT
- 1/4 C. CHOPPED CELERY
- HANDFUL RAISINS

TOFU EGGLESS SALAD
- 2 CAKES TOFU
- 1 C. COTTAGE CHEESE
- 2 STALKS CELERY, CHOPPED FINE
- HANDFUL NUTS OR RAISINS
- 2 t CURRY POWDER
- 1 APPLE DICED FINE

MIX WELL (serves 3)

ALTHOUGH THE WORD "GORP" HAS NOT YET MADE IT TO WEBSTER'S DICTIONARY, SOONER OR LATER, GORP BECOMES A STAPLE IN MOST HIKER'S AND CYCLIST'S LINGO.

ACCORDING TO HISTORICAL ACCOUNTS, THE DERIVATION OF THIS UNUSUAL TERM STEMS FROM THE ABBREVIATED — **G**OOD **O**LE' **R**AISINS and **P**EANUTS. KNOWN TO RESTORE LIFE IN ANY WEARY CYCLIST, GORP CONSISTS OF ANY HIGH ENERGY MIXTURE OF NUTS, SEEDS, DRIED FRUIT AND CHOCOLATE BITS (TRADITIONALLY M&M's). SOME DEDICATED GORP-LOVERS WOULD NOT EVEN THINK OF EXPLORING THE WILD OUTDOORS WITHOUT THEIR OWN, CONVENIENTLY LOCATED, GORP FIX.

THE INGREDIENTS OF GORP ALWAYS DEPEND ON THE IMAGINATION AND TASTE OF THE EATERS. ONE WAY TO PLEASE AN ENTIRE GROUP IS TO COMBINE ONE CUP OF EVERYONE'S FAVORITE GORP INGREDIENT. THE POSSIBILITIES ARE OF COURSE ENDLESS, BUT HERE ARE SOME IDEAS FOR THE BEGINNING GORPIE:

* Tropical * Fruit

DRIED APPLES
BANANA CHIPS
PINEAPPLE BITS
COCONUT FLAKES
PEANUTS
CHOCOLATE CHIP BITS.

* Squirrel's * Delight

SUNFLOWER SEEDS
WALNUTS
BRAZIL NUTS
CORN NUTS
PUMPKIN SEEDS
PEANUTS
M&Ms

* Mt. Monadnock * Munch

ALMONDS
PECANS
DATE PIECES
FILBERTS
DRIED APRICOTS
RAISINS
CASHEWS
CAROB PIECES.

WHAT A DAY! LET'S EAT!

AFTER A LONG DAY OF RIDING, FINDING A CAMPSIGHT AND SETTING UP CAMP, THERE IS LITTLE ENERGY LEFT TO MAKE AN ELABORATE MEAL — IT'S TIME FOR THE STEW THAT'S MADE CAMP COOKERY EASY — **THE ONE POT MEAL**. AS THE NAME INDICATES THE ONE POT MEAL IS MADE FROM START TO FINISH IN ONE POT. THERE IS NO MEASURING OF INGREDIENTS; THE STEW DEPENDS ENTIRELY ON YOU AND YOUR COMPANION'S TASTES AND APPETITES TO CREATE. EXPERIMENT WITH COMBINING INGREDIENTS; WHAT YOU THOUGHT WAS A MISTAKE MIGHT RESULT IN A DELICIOUS CONCOCTION!!

THE ONE POT MEAL HAS SIX BASIC COMPONENTS — PROTEIN, BASES (STARCH), SAUCES, SEASONINGS, VEGETABLES AND A TOPPING, THAT ALLOWS FOR INFINITE VARIETY. SIMPLY SELECT THE INGREDIENTS FROM EACH CATEGORY THAT YOU THINK MIGHT GO GOOD TOGETHER AND START COOKING. SOME IDEAS FOR COMBINATIONS:

✳ NOODLES · TUNA · TOMATO SAUCE · ONIONS · PEPPERS · CARROTS · CURRY POWDER · CHEESE ·

✳ RICE · COTTAGE CHEESE · BROCCOLI · MUSHROOMS · ONIONS · OREGANO · WALNUTS ·

✳ POTATO · YOGURT · CURRY SAUCE · CAULIFLOWER · CELERY · GARLIC · RAISINS · WHEAT GERM.

47.

THE ONE-POT MEAL

INGREDIENTS:

PROTEIN: TUNA, COMPLEMENTARY PROTEINS, DAIRY PRODUCTS, TOFU
BASES: (CARBOHYDRATES) PASTA, GRAINS, POTATOES, CORN, BREAD
SAUCES: CHEESE, TOMATO, CURRY, SOUR CREAM, YOGURT, SWEET-SOUR.
SEASONINGS: BE ADVENTUROUS !!
VEGGIES: ONIONS, PEPPERS, SQUASH, CARROTS !!, CABBAGE, TURNIP . . . . .
TOPPING: MELTED CHEESE (MMM!!) NUTS, WHEAT GERM, SPROUTS.

TO PREPARE:

① START COOKING BASE INGREDIENT IN WATER. WHEN HALF-COOKED, (SEE APPENDIX FOR COOKING TIMES) ADD VEGGIES. COVER AND STEAM.
② WHEN CARBOHYDRATES ARE ALMOST COOKED, ADD COOKED PROTEIN AND SEASONINGS. STIR GENTLY AND SIMMER.
③ ADD SAUCE AND MORE WATER IF STEW IS TOO THICK. SIMMER UNTIL VEGGIES ARE TENDER
④ ADD TOPPING AND SERVE !!

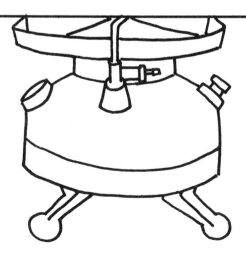

the SALAD BOWL

SALADS ARE THE ULTIMATE FREESTYLE MEAL, FOR THEY CAN BE MADE FROM ANY COMBINATION OF FRESH, COOKED OR MARINATED VEGETABLES. FOR THE BEGINNING CHEF, SALADS ARE A GREAT INTRODUCTION TO THE ART OF CULINARY EXPERIMENTATION — THERE'S NO RISK OF BURNING OR OVERCOOKING, (JUST DON'T SURPRISE ANYONE WITH RAW, HOT CHILI PEPPERS). MAKE THE SALAD A GROUP PROJECT BY HAVING A FEW PEOPLE CHOP VEGETABLES ~ EVERYONE LOVES TO NIBBLE AND IT SPEEDS UP THE SALAD PRODUCTION. TRY TOSSING ANY OF THE FOLLOWING INGREDIENTS FOR A CRUNCHY ACCOMPANIMENT TO ANY ONE POT MEAL.

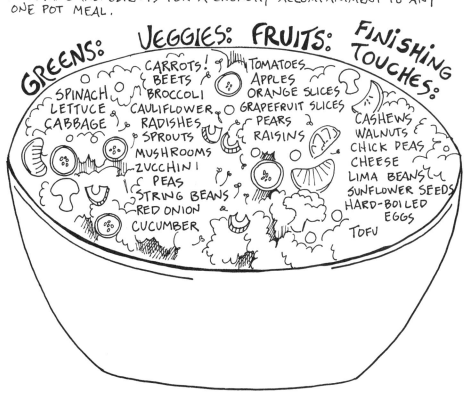

GREENS:
SPINACH
LETTUCE
CABBAGE

VEGGIES:
CARROTS!
BEETS
BROCCOLI
CAULIFLOWER
RADISHES
SPROUTS
MUSHROOMS
ZUCCHINI
PEAS
STRING BEANS
RED ONION
CUCUMBER

FRUITS:
TOMATOES
APPLES
ORANGE SLICES
GRAPEFRUIT SLICES
PEARS
RAISINS

FINISHING TOUCHES:
CASHEWS
WALNUTS
CHICK PEAS
CHEESE
LIMA BEANS
SUNFLOWER SEEDS
HARD-BOILED EGGS
TOFU

Tabouli

1C. DRY BULGUR
2C. WATER
2 MEDIUM ONIONS, FINELY CHOPPED
1C. CHOPPED MINT
3C. FINELY CHOPPED, FRESH PARSLEY
2 TOMATOES, DICED FINELY
1/4 C. OIL
JUICE OF 2 LEMONS
SALT

SOAK: BULGUR 2 HOURS
MIX: IN ONIONS
TOSS: IN MINT, PARSLEY, TOMATOES,
 OIL, LEMON JUICE, SALT.

Cool Slaw

1 SMALL HEAD CABBAGE (RED or WHITE)
1 C. CHOPPED CELERY
1 C. CHOPPED ONION
1/2 C. SHREDDED CARROT
1 C. CHOPPED APPLE
HANDFUL RAISINS OR WALNUTS

TOSS AND ADD:
1 C. YOGURT
1/2 C. MAYONNAISE
1/8 t. SALT
2 T. LEMON JUICE
2 T. HONEY
1 t. CELERY SEED

Fruit Salad

A CLEAN TASTE FOR YOUR
MOUTH AFTER DINNER

DICE, CUT, AND CHOP FRESH FRUITS
IN SEASON, AND TOSS WITH:

1 C. YOGURT
1 T. HONEY
2 T LEMON JUICE
2 t. CINNAMON
1/2 C. CHOPPED WALNUTS.

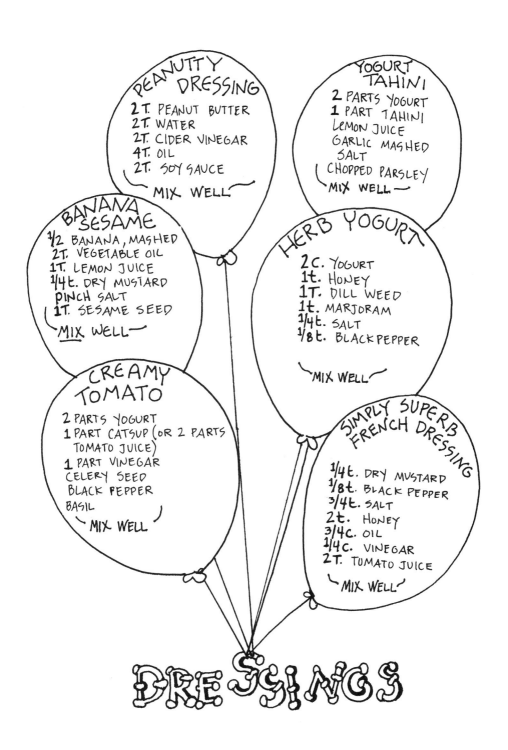

PEANUTTY DRESSING
2 T. PEANUT BUTTER
2 T. WATER
2 T. CIDER VINEGAR
4 T. OIL
2 T. SOY SAUCE
MIX WELL

YOGURT TAHINI
2 PARTS YOGURT
1 PART TAHINI
LEMON JUICE
GARLIC MASHED
SALT
CHOPPED PARSLEY
MIX WELL

BANANA SESAME
1/2 BANANA, MASHED
2 T. VEGETABLE OIL
1 T. LEMON JUICE
1/4 t. DRY MUSTARD
PINCH SALT
1 T. SESAME SEED
MIX WELL

HERB YOGURT
2 C. YOGURT
1 t. HONEY
1 T. DILL WEED
1 t. MARJORAM
1/4 t. SALT
1/8 t. BLACK PEPPER

MIX WELL

CREAMY TOMATO
2 PARTS YOGURT
1 PART CATSUP (OR 2 PARTS TOMATO JUICE)
1 PART VINEGAR
CELERY SEED
BLACK PEPPER
BASIL
MIX WELL

SIMPLY SUPERB FRENCH DRESSING
1/4 t. DRY MUSTARD
1/8 t. BLACK PEPPER
3/4 t. SALT
2 t. HONEY
3/4 c. OIL
1/4 c. VINEGAR
2 T. TOMATO JUICE
MIX WELL

DRESSINGS

SPROUTING ON THE ROAD

AS ALL GARDENERS CAN ATTEST TO, "SATISFYING YOUR INNER TUBE" TAKES ON SPECIAL MEANING WHEN YOU HAVE GROWN THE FOOD YOURSELF. WHILE YOUR PANNIERS ARE A RATHER LIMITED HABITAT FOR GROWING MOST VEGGIES, THEY ARE THE PERFECT HOME FOR NURTURING SEEDS INTO BABY SPROUTS, THAT ARE THEN READY FOR IMMEDIATE CONSUMPTION. SPROUTING REQUIRES MINIMUM EFFORT, YET, IN JUST THREE TO FOUR DAYS, SPROUTS CAN YIELD MAXIMUM SATISFACTION WHEN THEY ARE THROWN INTO SALADS, STEWS, SOUPS, SANDWICHES AND OMELETS.

ANY SEED CAN BE SPROUTED, BUT THE MOST POPULAR AND TASTEFUL ARE ALFALFA SEEDS AND MUNG BEAN SPROUTS. HOME-GROWN SPROUTS ALSO COST NEXT TO NOTHING COMPARED TO THE EXPENSIVE SUPERMARKET SPROUTS. (2T. SEEDS YIELDS ABOUT 2 C. SPROUTS).

FIRST SOAK 2T. MUNG BEANS OR ALFALFA SEEDS OVERNIGHT IN A WIDE-MOUTHED PLASTIC OR GLASS JAR. THE NEXT MORNING, DRAIN THE WATER THOROUGHLY THEN ALLOW YOUR SEEDS TO SPROUT USING ONE OF THE FOLLOWING METHODS:

CHEESECLOTH METHOD:

- PLACE THE SOAKED SEEDS ON TOP OF A PIECE OF CHEESE-CLOTH OR IN A CLEAN SOCK.
- ROLL IT UP AND PUT IT IN A BAGGIE AND STORE IN YOUR PANNIER SO IT WILL NOT GET CRUSHED
- TWICE A DAY RINSE AND DRAIN THE SPROUTS.
- EAT WHEN SPROUTS ARE FROM 1/2 TO 1" LONG.

JAR OR PLASTIC CONTAINER METHOD:

- COVER THE TOP OF THE JAR OR CONT WITH A PIECE OF CHEESECLOTH, MOSQUITO NETTING OR A SPECIAL LID FOR SPROUTING.

- SINCE THE SPROUTS CAN GROW IN THE DARK OR LIGHT, THEY CAN BE STORED INSIDE YOUR PANNIER OR LASHED ON TOP OF YOUR RACK BUT BE SURE TO KEEP THEM OUT OF DIRECT SUNLIGHT OR THEY WILL ROT.
- RINSE AND DRAIN THE SPROUTS THOROUGHLY TWICE DAILY, AND EAT WHEN SPROUTS ARE FROM 1/2" to 1" LONG (APPROXIMATELY 4-5 DAYS).

· POTATO · CORN · FISH ·

POTATO

1 CHOPPED ONION
2 C. WATER
1 t. SALT
5 MEDIUM-SIZE POTATOES
1 C. CARROTS
1 C. SHREDDED SPINACH
4 C. SCALDED MILK

SAUTÉ: VEGGIES (EXCEPT SPINACH)
ADD: WATER, BOIL
SIMMER: 15 MINUTES
ADD: SPINACH AND MILK AND SIMMER 5 MINUTES.

CORN

2 C. WATER
1/2 C. ONION CHOPPED
1/2 C. CHOPPED CELERY
1/2 C. DICED POTATO
1 C. RAW OR CANNED CORN
1/2 C. PARSLEY
4 C. MILK
1 t. SALT
PINCH GARLIC AND NUTMEG.

SAUTÉ: VEGGIES (EXCEPT CORN)
ADD: WATER, BOIL
ADD: CORN AND SPICES, SIMMER.
ADD: MILK, BRING TO SHORT BOIL.

FISH CHOWDER

IF CYCLING THROUGH LAKE COUNTRY OR BY THE SEA, THROW THE FRESHEST CATCH INTO THE POT!

TRUMANSBURG TUNA TANGO
serves 4   for Peter Kahn

1/2 C. CHOPPED ONION
1/4 C. CHOPPED GREEN PEPPER
1/2 lb. WHOLE WHEAT MACARONI
2 C. CHOPPED TOMATO
2 CANS TUNA, DRAINED
1 C. COLBY CHEESE, GRATED
1/2 C. WHEAT GERM
1 t. PARSLEY
1 CLOVE GARLIC
1/2 C. CHOPPED ALMONDS (TOPPING)

FOLLOW "ONE POT MEAL" DIRECTIONS

CAULIFLOWER CURRY
serves 4

6 C. WATER
2 C. BULGUR
2 ONIONS, CHOPPED
3 t. CURRY POWDER
2 C. DRY MILK
2 CANS TUNA
1 C. RAISINS
1/2 C. PEANUTS
COCONUT FLAKES (TOPPING)
1 SMALL HEAD CAULIFLOWER,
    CHOPPED.

FOLLOW "ONE-POT MEAL" DIRECTIONS

SLOPPY JOES
serves 6-8

4 T OIL
1 ONION CHOPPED
1 C. SOY BEAN FLAKES
1 C. RAW RICE
1 t. CHILI POWDER
1 t. SALT
3 C. WATER (BOILING)
  GRATED CHEESE.
SAUTÉ: VEGETABLES AND BEAN FLAKES
ADD: OTHER INGREDIENTS EXCEPT
    CHEESE
COVER: AND SIMMER 45 MINUTES
    UNTIL RICE IS DONE.
        SERVE
    ON BREAD OR BUNS. TOP WITH
        CHEESE.

Carrot Cashew Stew

A FAVORITE FOR RABBITS AND
REDHEADS
Serves 6

1/4 C. BUTTER OR OIL
1 1/2 C. CHOPPED ONIONS
4 C. GRATED CARROTS
3 oz. CAN TOMATO PASTE
1 C. CHOPPED PEPPER
6 C. WATER
1 C. CHOPPED APPLES
2 t. SALT
1/2 C. RAW RICE
1 C. RAISINS
1 C. CASHEWS
2 1/2 C. YOGURT OPTIONAL

SAUTÉ: ONIONS IN OIL THEN STIR IN
CARROTS, PEPPER AND TOMATO
PASTE.
ADD: WATER, APPLES AND SALT
BRING TO A BOIL: AND ADD RICE
COVER: AND SIMMER 45 MINUTES
ADD: RAISINS AND CASHEWS AND
SIMMER 5 MINUTES.

Spinach Surprise

Serves 4

2 C. COOKED RICE OR CRACKED WHEAT
3/4 C. GRATED CHEESE
2 EGGS
2 T. CHOPPED PARSLEY
1/2 t SALT
1 lb. SPINACH
2 ONIONS CHOPPED
2 T WHEAT GERM
1/2 C. WALNUTS, CHOPPED (that's the surprise!)

SAUTÉ: ONIONS AND WALNUTS IN OIL
ADD: COOKED GRAIN, CHEESE, EGGS
STIR IN: RAW SPINACH
TOP: WITH WHEAT GERM

55.

Pedal Pusher Broccoli Casserole

serves 3-4

Carrot Simmes

serves 4

2 ONIONS, CHOPPED
3T BUTTER OR MARGARINE
3C. CARROTS, DICED FINE
3C. APPLES, CHOPPED
1/4 C. CHOPPED PEANUTS
2T. HONEY
3 EGGS BEATEN
1/4 C WHEAT GERM   } MIX WELL
1 C. COTTAGE CHEESE
1T. CARAWAY
1T. DILL WEED

SAUTÉ: ONIONS, CARROTS, APPLES,
AND PEANUTS. (ADD WATER
TO STEAM IF NECESSARY).

ADD: EGG/CHEESE MIXTURE AND
SPICES.

SIMMER: 10 MINUTES AND SERVE WITH
RICE OR BREAD.

1/2 C. OIL
1 C. SOY FLAKES
2 ONIONS, CHOPPED
2 STALKS CELERY, CHOPPED.
1 BUNCH BROCCOLI
3 C. MILK
1/2 C. WHOLE WHEAT FLOUR
1/4 C. WHEAT GERM
1/2 C. SHREDDED CHEESE
1 CAN TUNA FISH
1/2 C. CHOPPED WALNUTS (OPTIONAL)

SAUTÉ: SOY FLAKES, ONION AND CELERY
IN OIL
ADD: BROCCOLI, MILK, AND WHOLE
WHEAT FLOUR, COOK UNTIL BROCCOLI
IS TENDER
STIR IN: WHEAT GERM AND TUNA FISH AND
ADD A LITTLE WATER IF NECES-
SARY, SIMMER 5 MINUTES.
TOP WITH: WALNUTS AND CHEESE

EVA'S KAULIFLOWER KASHA

serves 3

1 HEAD CAULIFLOWER
1C. KASHA (BUCKWHEAT GROATS)
1/2 ONION
1/2 lb. MUSHROOMS
2 CLOVES GARLIC
1C. MUENSTER CHEESE
1t. — PAPRIKA, PARSLEY, OREGANO
1T. SOY SAUCE
2C. WATER

SAUTÉ: ONIONS IN OIL WITH SPICES
ADD: REMAINING VEGGIES AND
1/4 C. WATER; ALLOW TO STEAM
A COUPLE MINUTES.
ADD: KASHA AND 2C. WATER,
BRING TO A BOIL, THEN
SIMMER AND ALLOW TO
COOK 40 MINUTES.
BEFORE SERVING: TOP WITH SOY SAUCE
AND CHEESE

NEVER VULGAR BULGAR

"serves 3 normal, 2 mega-hungry people"

"THIS WAS A DEEP-WOODS FAVORITE
ON MY NORTH CAROLINA OUTWARD
BOUND COURSES. I ALWAYS LABORED
FOR THE BULGAR TEXTURE AND SPICES
TO BE JUST RIGHT. BECAUSE SO MANY
PEOPLE HAD NEVER ENCOUNTERED
BULGAR IT WAS COMMONLY MISPRONOUNCED,
'OH NO, WE'RE HAVING VULGAR TONIGHT!'
BUT THIS RECIPE WAS NEVER VULGAR!"
— DAVID MORRISSEY MORIAH
ITHACA, N.Y.

1 C. BULGAR
1 SMALL ONION CHOPPED
1/2 lb. MUSHROOMS, SLICED
2 STALKS CELERY, CHOPPED
2 GREEN PEPPERS
3 1/2 OZ. CAN TOMATO PASTE
1/2 C. SESAME SEEDS
1/2 lb. CHEDDAR CHEESE
1 CLOVE GARLIC
2t. CUMIN, CHILI POWDER AND
OREGANO
2T. OIL OR BUTTER
2 1/2 C. WATER

SAUTÉ: ONIONS, CELERY, PEPPER, GARLIC
AND SPICES IN OIL. WHEN
VEGGIES ARE TENDER ADD
BULGAR.
ADD: WATER, TOMATO PASTE, MUSHROOM
AND STIR
COVER: AND SIMMER AT LOW BOIL FOR
15 MINUTES.
TOP: WITH CHEESE AND ALLOW
TO COOK 10 MORE MINUTES.

the HUMBLE BEAN

IN THE U.S. BEANS ARE ONE OF THOSE UNDERRATED FOODS THAT MANY PEOPLE BELIEVE ARE ONLY FOR VEGETARIANS. MORE AND MORE PEOPLE, HOWEVER, ARE DISCOVERING THE VIRTUES OF BEANS AND LEGUMES. FOR THE BUDGET CONSCIOUS CYCLE TOURIST AND OUTDOOR ENTHUSIAST, BEANS ARE AN EXCELLENT SOURCE OF FUEL AND NUTRIENTS SUCH AS: PROTEIN, IRON, AND B VITAMINS. BEANS AND LEGUMES ARE A VERSATILE FOOD AND EACH KIND — GARBANZO (CHICK PEA), LIMA, LENTIL, KIDNEY, SOYBEAN, SPLIT PEA, MUNG AND PEANUTS, TO NAME A FEW — HAVE THEIR OWN UNIQUE FLAVOR THAT CAN SATISFY A VARIETY OF PALATES. THE AMINO ACIDS IN BEANS ARE COMPLEMENTED BY THOSE IN GRAINS AND DAIRY PRODUCTS, AND ARE THUS A STAPLE IN A VEGETARIAN DIET; BUT BEANS CAN BE ADDED TO SOUPS, SALADS, CASSEROLES, STEWS AND EVEN BREADS, TO ENHANCE FLAVOR AND NUTRITIONAL QUALITY OF ANY MEAL.

BEANS ARE MOST ECONOMICAL WHEN PURCHASED DRY, THEN SOAKED AND COOKED (SEE APPENDIX) BUT IF YOU ARE SHORT ON TIME AND COOKING FUEL, MOST KINDS ARE AVAILABLE CANNED IN GROCERY STORES. IF YOUR TUMMY IS UNACCUSTOMED TO BEANS, IT IS BEST TO START WITH LENTILS, LIMAS, AND SPLIT PEAS WHICH ARE MORE EASILY DIGESTED.

LenTil Soup serves 4-6

3C. RAW LENTILS (soaked 1 hour)
7C. WATER
2t. SALT
1C. CHOPPED ONION
1C. CHOPPED CELERY
1C. CHOPPED CARROTS
2C. CHOPPED TOMATOES
1T. HONEY
1t. OREGANO
1t. NUTMEG
1t. BLACK PEPPER

BOIL: WATER, ADD LENTILS AND SALT
AND LET SIMMER ONE HOUR.
SAUTE: ONION, CELERY CARROTS, AND
TOMATOES, AND ADD TO COOKED
LENTILS. SIMMER 15 MINUTES.
ADD: HONEY AND SPICES, SIMMER 10 MINUTES
SERVE: WITH LOTS OF GRATED CHEESE
AND CORN FRITTERS ON THE SIDE.

Succotash Stew (serves 4-6)

2 C. CHOPPED ONIONS
1C. CHOPPED CELERY
6C. WARMED MILK
2C. CANNED OR FROZEN LIMA BEANS
2C. CANNED OR FROZEN CORN
1C. COOKED RICE
1/2t. SALT
1T. CHILI POWDER
1T. SOY SAUCE

SAUTE: VEGGIES IN OIL IN A BIG POT
UNTIL THEY ARE TENDER.
ADD: CORN AND COOK 5 MINUTES.
ADD LIMA BEANS, COOKED RICE, MIL
SOY SAUCE AND SPICES — SIMME
5 MINUTES.
SERVE: WITH CARROT FRITTERS.

TOFU STEW

TOFU IS A HIGHLY NUTRITIOUS FOOD MADE FROM SOYBEANS. IT IS RICH IN HIGH QUALITY PROTEIN BUT HAS NO FAT OR CHOLESTEROL— 8 OZ. OF TOFU HAS THE SAME AMOUNT OF USABLE PROTEIN AS 3 1/2 OZ OF STEAK. IT IS AN INEXPENSIVE, LOW-CALORIE FOOD THAT CAN BE ADDED TO ANY RECIPE AS AN EGG OR CHEESE SUBSTITUTE.

1/4 C. OIL
1 1/2 C. ONION CHOPPED
1 C. CARROTS, DICED FINE
1 C. CELERY, CHOPPED
2 t. GARLIC POWDER
2 CAKES TOFU, CUT INTO 1/2" CUBES.
1 1/2 C. ZUCCHINNI CHOPPED
2 TOMATOES, DICED
1 T. BASIL
1/2 t. PARSLEY
2 C. TOMATO JUICE OR 1 6 OZ. CAN TOMATO PASTE, DILUTED
1/3 C. SOY SAUCE
1 C. GRATED CHEESE

SAUTÉ: VEGGIES, BEGINNING WITH ONIONS AND ADDING OTHER VEGGIES AT 30 sec. INTERVALS.
ADD: TOFU, TOMATO JUICE, SOY SAUCE AND SIMMER 15 MINUTES.

Potatoes, Peas AND Tofu

— AN UNLIKELY, BUT DELICIOUS COMBINATION —
OIL OR BUTTER FOR FRYING
1 C. ONIONS, CHOPPED
1 T. CARRAWAY SEEDS
1/2 t. GARLIC POWDER
1 T. CURRY POWDER
1/2 t. CUMIN
1/2 t. SALT
3 POTATOES, SLICED
1/2 C. WATER
3 C. RAW PEAS (FRESH OR FROZEN)
2 CAKES TOFU (OR 4 EGGS IF TOFU IS NOT AVAILABLE)
1 C. GRATED CHEESE (OPTIONAL)

SAUTÉ: ONIONS AND SEASONINGS IN OIL.
ADD: POTATOES AND WATER AND ALLOW TO STEAM UNTIL POTATOES ARE TENDER.
ADD: MASHED TOFU AND REMAINING INGREDIENTS, STIR GENTLY AND ALLOW TO SIMMER 10 MINUTES.
TOP: WITH GRATED CHEESE AND SERVE.

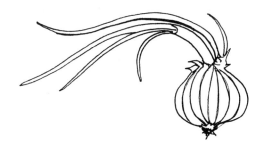

PASTA N' BEANS

serves 4-6

1 CAN CHICK PEAS
WATER
2 C. TOMATO SAUCE (16 OZ JAR)
½ t. BASIL
½ t. OREGANO
1 t. HONEY
2 T. BUTTER
1 C. SLICED MUSHROOMS
1 CAKE TOFU (MASHED)
3 T. PARMESAN CHEESE
1 C. FROZEN OR FRESH PEAS
1 PACKAGE GREEN NOODLES

SAUTÉ: MUSHROOMS AND SPICES
        IN BUTTER
ADD: TOFU AND PEAS AND
      COOK 5 MINUTES.
ADD: SAUCE, CHICK PEAS,
      CHEESE, HONEY AND
      SIMMER 5 MINUTES.
SERVE OVER HOT COOKED
GREEN NOODLES!

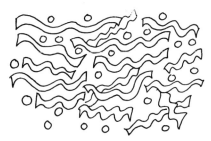

CABBAGETOWN'S CASHEW CHILI

AN ITHACA, N.Y
FAVORITE

serves 6

2-3 C. COOKED KIDNEY BEANS
  4 MEDIUM ONIONS, CHOPPED
  2 GREEN PEPPERS CHOPPED
  2 STALKS CELERY, CHOPPED
  3 CLOVES GARLIC CRUSHED
  1 t. BASIL
  1 t. OREGANO
  1 t. CUMIN
1 Qt. CANNED TOMATOES
PINCH BLACK PEPPER
½ - 1 C. CASHEWS
1 C. RAISINS
1 t. SALT
  2 CAKES TOFU (OPTIONAL)

SAUTÉ: VEGETABLES UNTIL
        TENDER.
ADD: CANNED TOMATOES AND
  SPICES AND SIMMER 10 MINUTES.
ADD: BEANS, CASHEWS AND
      RAISINS AND COOK 15 MINUTES.
SERVE: WITH GRATED CHEESE
  OR ADD PIECES OF TOFU FOR
  EXTRA PROTEIN.

MORE than MACARONI AND CHEESE

serves 4-6

4C. DRY MACARONI NOODLES
1C. CHOPPED ONIONS
1C. CHOPPED MUSHROOMS
1C. YOGURT (OR 1 CUP MILK)
1/2 C. SUNFLOWER SEEDS
1C. COTTAGE CHEESE
1C. SHARP CHEDDAR CHEESE
1C. WHEAT GERM OR SHREDDED WHEAT
1/4 C. PARSLEY
1t. SALT
1/2 t. PEPPER
1t. GARLIC.

COOK: MACARONI IN A LARGE POT WITH BOILING
WATER (3 TIMES THE VOLUME OF THE
PASTA BEING COOKED) 8-10 MINUTES.
DRAIN THE NOODLES AND TRANSFER
THEM TO SET IN A SEPARATE BOWL
WHILE YOU . . .

SAUTE: THE ONIONS, MUSHROOMS, SUNFLOWER
SEEDS AND SPICES IN OIL IN THE SAME
POT YOU USED TO COOK THE NOODLES.

ADD: YOGURT, COTTAGE CHEESE TO THE
VEGETABLES, STIR AND SIMMER.

MIX: MACARONI NOODLES AND VEGETABLES
AND ADD SHREDDED CHEESE; SIMMER
MIXTURE UNTIL CHEESE MELTS

TOP: WITH WHEAT GERM OR SHREDDED
WHEAT.

Pseudo Spanish Rice

serves 4

1 1/2 C. CHOPPED ONION
2C. CHOPPED GREEN PEPPER
1C. GARBANZO BEANS (CANNED)
16 OZ. CAN TOMATO PASTE
1 3/4 C. RAW BROWN RICE
1/4 C. OIL
1C. GRATED CHEESE
2 TOMATOES, CHOPPED
1/2 t. SALT
1t. OREGANO
1t BASIL
2t GARLIC POWDER

SAUTE: IN LARGE POT—ONIONS, GARLIC
SPICES AND PEPPER IN OIL.

ADD: RAW RICE, TOMATO PASTE, AND
3 CUPS WATER, BRING TO A BOIL
THEN SIMMER 20 MINUTES.

ADD: TOMATOES AND BEANS (AND MORE
WATER IF NECESSARY) SIMMER
10 MINUTES.

STIR: MIXTURE AND SERVE TOPPED WITH
GRATED CHEESE

TACOS

POTATO EGG ← the fillings → GARBANZO AND SUNFLOWER SEED

POTATO EGG

8 TACO SHELLS

5 EGGS
2 MEDIUM POTATOES, DICED
2 ONIONS, CHOPPED
1 C. SHARP CHEDDAR CHEESE, GRATED.
2 GREEN PEPPERS, CHOPPED
1/2 C. WALNUTS CHOPPED, (OPTIONAL)
DASH: CUMIN, BLACK PEPPER, CURRY GARLIC

SAUTÉ: ONIONS, PEPPERS, AND POTATOES IN OIL UNTIL TENDER.

ADD: BEATEN EGGS, CHEESE, OPTIONAL WALNUTS AND SPICES AND SIMMER UNTIL EGGS ARE COOKED AND CHEESE IS MELTED.

SPOON: FILLING INTO SHELLS AND ADD TOPPING.

GARBANZO AND SUNFLOWER SEED

8 TACO SHELLS

1 6 OZ. CAN TOMATO PASTE
1 C. SUNFLOWER SEEDS
1 LARGE ONION, CHOPPED.
2 GREEN PEPPERS, CHOPPED
1 C. or 1 CAN GARBANZO BEANS
1 t. CUMIN
2 t. GARLIC POWDER
2 t. CHILI POWDER
BLACK PEPPER to TASTE

SAUTÉ: ONIONS, GREEN PEPPERS AND SUNFLOWER SEEDS IN OIL UNTIL VEGGIES ARE TENDER.

ADD: TOMATO PASTE, GARBANZO BEANS, AND SEASONINGS.

SPOON: FILLING INTO SHELLS.

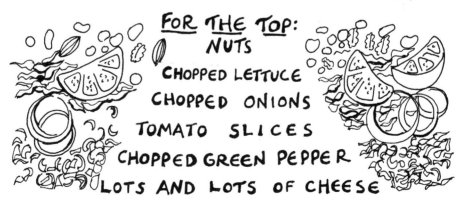

FOR THE TOP:
NUTS
CHOPPED LETTUCE
CHOPPED ONIONS
TOMATO SLICES
CHOPPED GREEN PEPPER
LOTS AND LOTS OF CHEESE

MANGIA!

Egg plant Parmesan
serves 4

Minestrone
(BIG SOUP) serves 4-6

1 lb. EGGPLANT, UNPEELED
1 lb. CAN TOMATOES OR 5 CHOPPED TOMATOES
1 ONION, DICED
1 GREEN PEPPER, DICED
1 C. CORNMEAL OR WHOLE WHEAT FLOUR
OIL FOR FRYING
3/4 C. PARMESAN OR CHEDDAR CHEESE
OREGANO, BASIL, CUMIN, CELERY SEED
OPTIONAL - CRUMBLED CAKE OF TOFU.

SLICE: EGGPLANT INTO 1/2" SLICES
DIP: SLICES INTO WATER, THEN INTO
CORNMEAL AND SAUTÉ BOTH SLICES
UNTIL TENDER. ADD OIL TO PREVENT
BURNING. PUT ASIDE.
SAUTÉ: ONION AND GREEN PEPPER UNTIL
ONIONS ARE TRANSPARENT.
STIR IN: TOMATOES, SEASONINGS AND OP-
-TIONAL CRUMBLED TOFU.
SIMMER: 5 -10 MINUTES
LAYER EGGPLANT INTO PAN AND SPOON
MIXTURE OVER IT AND THEN ADD
THE CHEESE... AND .. ALLOW..
TO MELT.. ...MMMMM!

2 1/2 C. GARBANZO BEANS
1/2 C. DRY PASTA
1 C. FRESH, CHOPPED TOMATOES
1 LARGE ONION CHOPPED.
1 C. DICED CARROTS
1 C. MINCED CELERY
1 C. CHOPPED EGGPLANT
1 C. CHOPPED PEPPER
1 CAN TOMATO PASTE
4 C. WATER
BASIL, OREGANO, GARLIC, PEPPER

SAUTÉ: ONIONS, PEPPER, GARLIC AND
SPICES IN OIL.
ADD: OTHER VEGETABLES AND ALLOW
TO STEAM IN SMALL AMOUNT
WATER.
STIR IN: BEANS, ADD STOCK AND
SIMMER 15 -20 MINUTES.
ADD: TOMATOES AND PASTE AND
SIMMER 5 MINUTES
ADD: SPICE AND TOP WITH CHEESE.

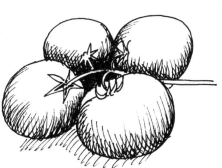

PASTA

WHEN IT'S LATE IN THE DAY AND YOU DON'T LIKE TO EVEN THINK ABOUT MAKING DINNER, THEN IT'S TIME FOR THE EASY AND DEPENDABLE CROWD-PLEASER— PASTA! BUT BE CAREFUL! WITHOUT A LITTLE TENDER LOVING CARE, DELICATE NOODLES ARE EASILY OVERCOOKED!! ITALIANS PREFER IT "AL DENTE," WHICH MEANS RESISTANT TO THE BITE.

2 C. OR 1/2 lb. UNCOOKED PASTA YIELDS 4 C. COOKED PASTA
BOIL: 8 CUPS WATER WITH 2 t. SALT
SLOWLY, POUR IN: PASTA, KEEP WATER BOILING UNCOVERED.
STIR: OCCASIONALLY WITH FORK TO KEEP PASTA FROM STICKING.
DRAIN: AND SERVE WITH SAUCE.

Mama Orazietti's Tomato Sauce

1 ONION, DICED
1 CLOVE GARLIC, CHOPPED
1 GREEN PEPPER, DICED
3 T. OIL
SEA SALT
2 t. BASIL
1 t. OREGANO
1 t. CUMIN
1 t. CHILI POWDER
} SAUTÉ

1 CAN TOMATOES OR 4 FRESH TOMATOES CHOPPED
1 6 OZ. CAN TOMATO PASTE
WATER, TO SAUCE CONSISTENCY
} ADD TO VEGGIES AND SIMMER

OPTIONAL EXTRAS!
1/2 lb. CHOPPED MUSHROOMS
1/2 C. GRATED PARMESAN
2 CAKES CUBED TOFU
1 CAN TUNA FISH.

64.

SPAGHETTI ALLA CARBONARA

6 EGGS
2 C. PARMESAN CHEESE
2 LARGE ONIONS CHOPPED
6 T. OIL
SALT, PEPPER

BEAT: EGG AND CHEESE, SET ASIDE.
COOK: SPAGHETTI IN BOILING WATER (8-10 MINUTES) SET ASIDE.
SAUTÉ: ONIONS IN OIL UNTIL TENDER.
ADD: SPAGHETTI TO ONIONS, THEN STIR IN EGG/CHEESE MIXTURE AND CONTINUE TO STIR ON LOW HEAT UNTIL EGG IS COOKED AND CHEESE IS MELTED

FETTUCINE FACILE (easy)

1 CAN CREAM OF MUSHROOM SOUP
1 1/2 C. PARMESAN CHEESE
1/2 C. BUTTER
2 EGGS BEATEN
DASH SALT, PEPPER
2 t. GARLIC POWDER
1 lb. FETTUCINE NOODLES

COOK: NOODLES (10 MINUTES) SET ASIDE
HEAT: CREAM SOUP ON LOW HEAT
ADD: CHEESE SLOWLY
STIR: 5 MINUTES AND ADD BUTTER UNTIL MELTED
ADD: BEATEN EGGS AND STIR IN SEASONINGS
SERVE: OVER HOT COOKED NOODLES

Conchiglie Tutto Giardino

"PASTA WITH THE WHOLE GARDEN"

1 1/2 C. SLICED CARROTS
2 LARGE SLICED ONIONS,
7 MEDIUM TOMATOES CHOPPED.
1 ZUCCHINI SLICED.
6 OZ. TOMATO PASTE
1/2 C GRATED PARMESAN CHEESE
1 LARGE BELL PEPPER
2 T. BASIL
1 T. GARLIC
1 t. BLACK PEPPER
1 T. WHOLE WHEAT FLOUR
1 1/2 LBS. PASTA.

SAUTÉ: ONIONS, PEPPER, CARROT AND SEASONINGS IN OIL UNTIL TENDER.
ADD: TOMATOES, TOMATO PASTE, FLOUR, ZUCCHINI AND ENOUGH WATER FOR A SAUCE CONSISTENCY
SIMMER: 10 MINUTES AND STIR IN PARMESAN CHEESE.
SERVE: HOT OVER COOKED PASTA

Ronen's Cross-Continental Macaroon 𝒞 𝒞 𝒞 𝒞 𝒞

A "MACAROON," ACCORDING TO THE INVENTOR OF THIS PSEUDO-LASAGNE DISH, IS ANY RICH AND HEARTY PASTA MEAL GUARANTEED TO SATISFY EVEN THE MOST RAVENOUS HUNGER. THIS PARTICULAR "MACAROON" WAS A FAVORITE ON HIS 7,000 MILE CROSS-CONTINENTAL BICYCLE TOUR.

10-12 OZ. FLAT NOODLES OR ELBOW MACARONI
2 ONIONS CHOPPED
2 GREEN PEPPERS, CHOPPED
1 SMALL JAR TOMATO SAUCE OR 1 1/2 C. HOME-MADE SAUCE.
1/2 lb. MUSHROOMS, SLICED
1 1/2 C. RICOTTA CHEESE
1/2 C. MOZZARELLA CHEESE
1 t. EACH: GARLIC POWDER, BLACK PEPPER, OREGANO

COOK: NOODLES IN WATER, DRAIN AND SET ASIDE.
SAUTÉ: ONIONS, MUSHROOMS, GREEN PEPPER AND SPICES IN OIL.
MIX: SAUTÉED VEGGIES, COOKED NOODLES AND CHEESES IN A LARGE POT. STIR GENTLY AND ALLOW TO SIMMER 10 MINUTES.

IF YOU ARE TOURING IN A REMOTE AREA, THERE MIGHT BE DAYS WHEN YOU WILL HAVE NO CHOICE BUT TO BUY FOOD AT A SMALL GENERAL STORE THAT HAS A VERY LIMITED SUPPLY OF STAPLES AND CANNED FOODS. BUT, ALAS, THINK POSITIVELY, AND REMEMBER THE HIKER'S AND CYCLIST'S CREED:

ANYTHING TASTES GOOD WHEN YOU'RE REALLY HUNGRY!

SO CONTROL YOUR CRAVING FOR FRESH VEGETABLES, FRUITS, CHEESE GRANOLA AND TOFU (THERE IS ALWAYS TOMORROW) AND FIX YOURSELF A:

CORN & BEAN STEW (serves 4)

2 CANS CORN
2 CANS LIMA BEANS
1 CAN TOMATO SOUP
1 C. DICED POTATOES (CANNED OR FRESH)
1 C. CHOPPED ONIONS (CANNED OR FRESH)
1 t. BLACK PEPPER, CHILI POWDER, BASIL.

SAUTÉ: ONIONS AND POTATOES IN OIL
ADD: TOMATO SOUP AND SIMMER UNTIL POTATOES ARE TENDER
ADD: REMAINING INGREDIENTS AND SIMMER 10 MINUTES

TUNA STEW ON TOAST
(serves 4)

1 CAN CREAM OF MUSHROOM SOUP
1/2 C. MILK
1 CAN TUNA
1 CAN DRAINED GREEN PEAS
2 HARD BOILED EGGS
4 SLICES BREAD

HEAT: ALL INGREDIENTS EXCEPT BREAD.
SERVE: ON BREAD FRIED IN BUTTER.

KRAFT N' SHROOMS

serves 2-3

2 PACKAGES KRAFT MACARONI
   AND CHEESE DINNERS.
1 CAN TUNA FISH
1 CAN MUSHROOMS
1 CAN WHOLE TOMATOES
PREPARE: MACARONI ACCORDING TO
   DIRECTIONS
ADD: TUNA FISH, MUSHROOMS AND
   TOMATOES.

QUICK CHILI

serves 4

1 CAN KIDNEY BEANS
1 CAN TOMATO PASTE
1 CAN GARBANZO BEANS
1 C. RAW RICE (WHITE OR BROWN)
1 C. SLICED ONIONS (CANNED OR
   FRESH)
1 T. CHILI POWDER
1 t. CUMIN, BLACK PEPPER, GARLIC
   POWDER
3½ C. WATER

SAUTÉ: ONIONS IN BUTTER
ADD: WATER AND TOMATO PASTE,
   BRING TO A BOIL AND ADD
   RICE THEN—
SIMMER: INGREDIENTS UNTIL
   RICE IS COOKED
ADD: BEANS AND SPICES,
   SIMMER 5 MINUTES

GAP MT. GLOP

serves 2-3

1 CAN CORN
1 CAN PEAS
1 CAN CREAM OF MUSHROOM SOUP
2 C. MASHED POTATOES (MADE
   FROM SCRATCH OR FROM A BOX)
1 t. BASIL, OREGANO, BLACK PEPPER

PREPARE: MASHED POTATOES —
   FROM SCRATCH: DICE 4
   POTATOES, BOIL IN WATER
   20 MINUTES. DRAIN WATER.
   MASH WITH A FORK AND
   ADD ¼ C. MILK AND 1
   T. BUTTER
   FROM THE BOX: FOLLOW
   COOKING DIRECTIONS
ADD: REMAINING INGREDIENTS
   AND SIMMER 10 MINUTES.

BADLANDS BREW

2 CANS GREEN BEANS
1 CAN CREAM OF TOMATO SOUP
2 SMALL CANS MUSHROOMS
1 CAN TUNA FISH
½ CUP BREAD CRUMBS
DILL WEED, CARAWAY
serves 2-3

MIX AND HEAT: ALL INGREDIENTS
TOP: WITH BREAD CRUMBS.

FRITTERS

FRITTERS ARE BASICALLY A CROSS BETWEEN A PANCAKE AND AN OMELET AND ARE FRIED IN EXTRA OIL TO GIVE THEM A CRISPY AND SATISFYING FLAVOR. THEY CAN BE MADE QUICKLY WHILE DINNER IS COOKING, BUT DON'T EAT THEM ALL BEFORE ITS DONE, FOR THEY ARE GREAT FOR SOAKING UP THAT LAST BITE.

CORN FRITTERS (serves 4-6)

2 C. CORN (CANNED OR FROZEN)
2 C. MILK
2 EGGS
2 t BAKING POWDER
2 C. WHOLE WHEAT FLOUR
1 C. CHOPPED CHEDDAR CHEESE

MIX: ALL INGREDIENTS
FRY: BY SPOONFUL ONTO HOT OILED PAN

CARROT FRITTERS (serves 4-6)

1 1/2 lbs. CARROTS (GRATED)
1 C. WHOLE WHEAT FLOUR
1 t. BAKING POWDER
1 EGG BEATEN
1/4 t. SALT
1/4 C. RAISINS
1/2 C. COTTAGE CHEESE

MIX: ALL INGREDIENTS
FRY: BY THE SPOONFUL ONTO HOT, OILED PAN.

NUT CAKES (serves 4-6)

1/2 lb. CASHEWS, CHOPPED FINE
1/2 lb. WALNUTS, CHOPPED FINE
1 C. COOKED RICE
1 C. GRATED CHEESE
1/2 C. ONION CHOPPED
3 EGGS BEATEN
1 t. SALT
1/2 C. WHOLE WHEAT FLOUR

MIX: ALL INGREDIENTS
FRY: BY SPOONFUL ONTO HOT OILED PAN

RICE CAKES

2 C. COOKED BROWN RICE
1/4 C. OIL
1 EGG
1 t. SALT
1/2 C. WHOLE WHEAT FLOUR

MIX: ALL INGREDIENTS
FRY: BY SPOONFUL ONTO HOT PAN

APPLE FRITTERS

1 3/4 C. WHOLE WHEAT FLOUR
3 t. BAKING POWDER
1/2 t. SALT
1 EGG BEATEN
1 C. MILK (OR COTTAGE CHEESE)
1 T. HONEY
1 T. OIL
8 SMALL APPLES CHOPPED
OIL FOR FRYING
CINNAMON, NUTMEG

MIX: ALL INGREDIENTS
FRY: BY SPOONFUL ONTO HOT PAN

SOY FRITTERS

2 C. COOKED SOY FLAKES
4 T. OIL
1 C. WHEAT GERM
1/2 C. WHOLE WHEAT FLOUR
2 EGGS BEATEN
2 T. SOY SAUCE

MIX: ALL INGREDIENTS
FRY: BY SPOONFUL ONTO HOT PAN

ZUCCHINI CAKES

3 MEDIUM ZUCCHINI (GRATED)
1 ONION MINCED
1 CLOVE GARLIC, MINCED
2 EGGS, BEATEN
1 C. WHOLE WHEAT FLOUR
1/4 C. PARSLEY

MIX: ALL INGREDIENTS
FRY: BY SPOONFUL ONTO HOT OILED
PAN.

BASIC BACKWOODS BAKING

FOR MANY PEOPLE, MAKING BREAD, EVEN IN THE CONVENIENCE OF THEIR OWN KITCHEN, SEEMS LIKE AN INVOLVED PROJECT THAT REQUIRES AN ENTIRE AFTERNOON. ACTUALLY, IT IS A SIMPLE AND MEDITATIVE PROCESS WITH DELICIOUS RESULTS THAT HAVE NO COMPARISON. IF YOU THINK YOU ENJOY THE AROMA OF BREAD BAKING IN A WARM HOME, WAIT UNTIL ITS FUMES REACH YOUR NOSE IN CAMP WHEN YOU'RE REALLY HUNGRY! WHILE MANY CAMPERS ARE ADDICTED TO BAKING, I CHOOSE TO BAKE ONLY WHEN I WANT TO REALLY TREAT MYSELF. YOU NEED NO EXTRA EQUIPMENT TO BAKE AND CAN EITHER USE THE FIRE PIT OR THE DOUBLE BOILER METHOD FOR BAKING.

FIRE PIT BAKING

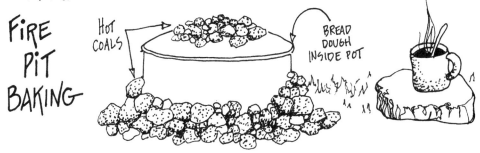

① MAKE A BED OF COALS FROM A BURNED DOWN FIRE.
② PLACE A FEW SMALL ROCKS ON THE COALS SO THE POT MAY REST ABOVE THE HEAT SLIGHTLY.
③ COVER POT (WITH DOUGH INSIDE) AND PLACE HOT COALS OR START A SMALL TWIGGY FIRE ON THE LID.
④ AS THE COALS COOL, REPLENISH THEM WITH HOT ONES. IF THE COALS ARE VERY HOT, COOKING TIME SHOULD BE THE SAME AS A REGULAR OVEN.
   • A COFFEE CAN COVERED WITH TIN FOIL MAY ALSO BE USED AS A STOVE •

DOUBLE BOILER METHOD
(BEST FOR SWEET BREADS)

① ADD ABOUT 1/2 C. → 2/3 C WATER TO YOUR LARGEST POT.

② PUT THE DOUGH INTO A SMALLER POT AND SNUGGLE IT INSIDE THE LARGER POT.

③ PUT LIDS ON BOTH POTS AND PLACE THEM ON THE STOVE.

④ AS THE WATER BOILS, THE STEAM WILL COOK THE CAKE. REPLACE THE WATER AS IT BOILS DOWN.

NOTE: THIS DOUBLE BOILER METHOD ONLY HEATS TO APPROXIMATELY 200° – 250°, AND THEREFORE TAKES LONGER TO BAKE BREADS AND CAKES.

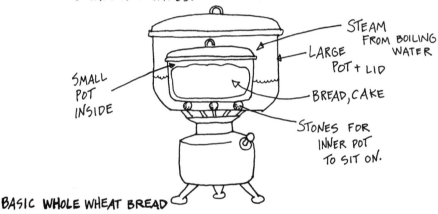

STEAM FROM BOILING WATER

LARGE POT + LID

SMALL POT INSIDE

BREAD, CAKE

STONES FOR INNER POT TO SIT ON.

BASIC WHOLE WHEAT BREAD

4 C. WHOLE WHEAT FLOUR
1 t. SALT
1/4 C. SHORTENING OR OIL
1 T YEAST

2 T MOLASSES OR HONEY
1/2 C. POWDERED MILK
4 t. BAKING POWDER
1 1/4 C. WARM WATER

DISSOLVE: YEAST IN LUKEWARM WATER AND ALLOW TO SIT 5 MINUTES.

STIR IN: SUGAR, SALT AND BAKING POWDER. SLOWLY STIR IN FLOUR AND POWDERED MILK.

BEAT: DOUGH VIGOROUSLY 2-3 MINUTES UNTIL DOUGH IS ELASTIC (ADD MORE FLOUR IF DOUGH IS WATERY).

KNEAD: FOR 10 MINUTES AND ALLOW TO RISE 1-2 HOURS, COVERED.

PUNCH: DOUGH DOWN AND LET IT RISE UNTIL IT SPRINGS BACK WHEN YOU STICK YOUR FINGER IN IT.

PLACE: DOUGH IN SMALL POT OR PAN AND BAKE COVERED BY EITHER STEAM OR HOT COAL METHOD, 40-50 MINUTES.

THE INDESTRUCTIBLE: LOGAN BREAD

LOGAN BREAD'S HISTORICAL ROOTS DATE BACK TO 1950 WHEN GORDON HERREID BROUGHT IT WITH HIM ON HIS CLIMB TO THE TOP OF MT. LOGAN (19,850 FEET IN ELEVATION IN THE SOUTHWEST YUKON TERRITORY OF CANADA). ITS MAIN VIRTUES ARE ITS DURABILITY AND DENSITY, WHICH MAKES IT GREAT FOR BIKERS AND BACK-PACKERS WHO OFTEN NEED A CONCEN-TRATED SOURCE OF CALORIES. YOU CAN SOFTEN IT BY DUNKING IT IN MILK OR HOT DRINKS OR JUST ENJOY GNAWING ON IT SLOWLY.

Cheesy Bread

2 C. WATER
7 C. WHOLE WHEAT FLOUR
1 C. HONEY
2 1/4 C. DRY MILK
1 T. BAKING POWDER
1 T. SALT
1 2/3 C. BROWN SUGAR
1/2 C. MOLASSES
1/2 C. OIL
3/4 C. WHEAT GERM
OPTIONAL: 1 C. — DRIED FRUITS OR NUTS

MIX: ALL INGREDIENTS WELL
PUT INTO: GREASED 10 x 14 INCH
         PAN OR DEEP FRY PAN
BAKE: FOR 1 HOUR AND 15 MINUTES
     USING COAL FIRE METHOD OR
     IN 300° OVEN.
CUT: INTO 20 SQUARES
ALLOW TO DRY AND COOL THOROUGHLY
THEN STORE IN PLASTIC BAGS. THIS
CRUNCHY BREAD WILL KEEP FOR
2 WEEKS!

3/4 C. WARM MILK OR WATER ⎫
1/4 C. OIL   ⎬ Ⓐ
1 T. RAW HONEY   ⎪
3 EGGS BEATEN   ⎭

2 1/2 C. WHOLE WHEAT FLOUR ⎫
1 T. DRY YEAST   ⎪
1 1/2 t. SALT   ⎬ Ⓑ
1/4 C. SUNFLOWER SEEDS   ⎪
2 C. GRATED CHEESE   ⎭

MIX: INGREDIENTS IN Ⓐ
MIX: INGREDIENTS IN Ⓑ
MIX: Ⓐ AND Ⓑ, KNEAD UNTIL
     SMOOTH
COVER: AND LET RISE 45 MINUTES.
BAKE: FOR 45 MINUTES USING
     COAL FIRE METHOD OR IN
     375° OVEN.

Pitcher Mt. Blueberry Bread

AFTER SPENDING AN ENTIRE DAY EATING AND PICKING BLUEBERRIES ON TOP OF PITCHER MOUNTAIN IN STODDARD, NEW HAMPSHIRE, I EXPERIMENTED WITH WAYS TO USE THE 4 QUARTS OF BERRIES THAT I HAD PICKED. FOR DAYS EVERYTHING I PREPARED — SALADS, CEREAL, OMELETS, AND EVEN SOUPS — WAS SPECKLED WITH BLUE, WHICH RESULTED IN A TEMPORARY GLOWING, PURPLE SMILE FOR ALL WHO INDULGED IN MY CONCOCTIONS.

ONE OF MY FAVORITES WAS THE FOLLOWING BREAD IN WHICH THE BLUEBERRIES EXPLODE WHILE THE BREAD IS BAKING AND BLEND WONDERFULLY WITH THE YELLOW CORN MEAL.

1/4 C. YELLOW CORN MEAL
1 C. BOILING WATER
1 T. OIL
1/4 C. MOLASSES
1 T ACTIVE YEAST
1 EGG, BEATEN
1/4 C. LUKEWARM WATER
3 C. WHOLE WHEAT OR WHITE FLOUR
2 C. BLUEBERRIES

STIR: CORNMEAL INTO BOILING WATER UNTIL MIXTURE THICKENS. REMOVE FROM HEAT AND ADD OIL, MOLASSES AND EGG.

DISSOLVE: YEAST, ADD TO CORN MEAL

ADD: REMAINING FLOUR AND KNEAD 10 MINUTES.

COVER: AND LET DOUGH RISE UNTIL DOUBLED IN BULK.

PUNCH: DOUGH DOWN FLAT AND SPRINKLE BLUEBERRIES ON TOP.

ROLL UP: DOUGH WITH BLUEBERRIES INSIDE

COVER: AND LET RISE AGAIN (45 MINUTES)

BANANA-NUT BREAD

1/3 C. HONEY
1/2 C. OIL
3 MEDIUM, RIPE BANANAS-MASHED
2 EGGS, WELL BEATEN
1 t. VANILLA
1 1/2 C. WHOLE WHEAT FLOUR
1/2 C. WHEAT GERM
2 t. BAKING POWDER
1/2 t. SALT
1/2 t. CINNAMON
1/2 C. CHOPPED NUTS
1/2 C. RAISINS

MIX: HONEY AND OIL
STIR IN: BANANAS, VANILLA AND EGGS.
COMBINE: REMAINING INGREDIENTS
   AND STIR UNTIL MIXED.

BAKE: FOR 1 HOUR, 10 MINUTES USING
   DOUBLE BOILER METHOD OR IN
   325° OVEN

ANADAMA BREAD

1 C. SCALDED MILK
1 1/2 C. WATER
1 C. YELLOW CORNMEAL
1/4 C. OIL
1/2 C. MOLASSES
2 t. SALT
2 CAKES YEAST
2 C. UNBLEACHED FLOUR
4 C. WHOLE WHEAT FLOUR

COMBINE: HOT MILK AND 1 C. BOILING
   WATER AND SLOWLY ADD THE
   CORNMEAL
ADD: OIL MOLASSES AND SALT
ALLOW TO SIT: UNTIL MIXTURE IS
   LUKEWARM.
MIX: YEAST WITH 1/2 C. WARM WATER
   AND LET SIT 5 MINUTES, THEN
   STIR IT INTO CORNMEAL MIXTURE.
BEAT IN: FLOUR AND KNEAD UNTIL SMOOTH.
ALLOW TO RISE: COVERED UNTIL DOUBLED,
   ABOUT 1 1/2 HOURS
KNEAD: AGAIN AND DIVIDE INTO 2
   LOAVES AND ALLOW TO RISE
   UNTIL DOUBLE AGAIN.

BAKE: FOR 1 HOUR IN COAL FIRE OR
   IN 375° OVEN

IF, IN THE MIDDLE OF A STARRY EVENING, YOU SEE CONSTELLATIONS IN MYRIADS OF CIRCULAR SHAPES AND ENVISION STRANDS OF MOZZARELLA DANGLING FROM YOUR MOUTH, AND JUICY TOMATO SAUCE STICKING ON YOUR LIPS, THEN YOU ARE DEFINITELY SUFFERING FROM PIZZA DEPRIVATION. HERE IS A SIMPLE RECIPE THAT WILL CURE EVEN THE MOST SERIOUS CASE:

THE DOUGH
1 1/2 T. ACTIVE DRY YEAST
1/2 C. WARM WATER
1 1/2 C. WHOLE WHEAT FLOUR
1 T. OIL

DISSOLVE: YEAST IN WARM WATER.
STIR IN: FLOUR AND OIL. KNEAD ABOUT THREE MINUTES.
ALLOW TO RISE UNTIL DOUBLE IN BULK.
SPREAD: DOUGH OVER OILED FRY PAN.
BAKE 10 MINUTES IN COAL OVEN, THEN REMOVE AND ADD TOPPING.

TOPPING:
- SMALL JAR OF TOMATO SAUCE
- GARLIC, OREGANO, BASIL
- MUCHO MOZZARELLA CHEESE
- PARMESAN CHEESE
- STIR FRIED SELECTION OF YOUR FAVORITE TOPPINGS: MUSHROOMS, ONIONS, BROCCOLI, PEPPERS

SPREAD: SAUCE ON CRUST.
SPRINKLE: SPICES ON TOP.
SPREAD: AN EVEN LAYER OF CHEESE AND VEGETABLES.
BAKE: PIZZA FOR ANOTHER 10-15 MINUTES. (FIRE PIT METHOD)

ONE EVENING, THE PIZZA FEVER BECAME SO ACUTE FOR ALL TEN MEMBERS OF OUR GROUP THAT WE COULD NOT WAIT TO MAKE OUR OWN PIZZA AND WERE FORCED TO RESORT TO EMERGENCY PROCEDURES. LUCKILY, OUR CAMPSITE WAS NEAR A PHONE WHERE WE CALLED LUIGI'S PIZZA, AND WITHIN 20 MINUTES THE LIFESAVING TRUCK ARRIVED. WE FRANTICALLY EMERGED FROM THE WOODS AND RAN TOWARDS THE TRUCK TO OUR AWAITING LARGE PIZZA WITH THE WORKS. AFTER DEVOURING ONE PIECE WE WERE INSTANTLY CURED AND COULD CALMLY RETURN TO OUR SLEEPING BAGS.

QUICHE

GOES TO THE WOODS

BEFORE I BEGAN A HIKING EXPEDITION FOR 5 WEEKS IN THE WIND RIVERS OF WYOMING WITH THE NATIONAL OUTDOOR LEADERSHIP SCHOOL, I ENVISIONED A DIET OF LOTS OF BEANS, RICE AND CHEESE. HOWEVER, AFTER WE ALL LEARNED THE BASICS OF BACKWOODS BAKING, I ATTEMPTED TO BAKE A WILDFLOWER QUICHE WITH A WHOLE WHEAT CRUST. THE QUICHE, ALONG WITH A FRESH GREENS SALAD AND BROWN RICE, WAS A SUCCESS AND STARTED MY COOKING GROUP ON ITS WAY TO THE MOST EXQUISITE GOURMET BANQUETS.

THE CRUST:

2 C. WHOLE WHEAT FLOUR
1 t. SALT
1/2 C. BUTTER OR MARGARINE
1/4 C. WATER

MIX: FLOUR AND SALT
ADD: SLICES OF BUTTER AND MIX TOGETHER WITH A FORK
ADD: WATER AND MIX UNTIL DOUGHY CONSISTENCY
FLATTEN: INTO PANCAKE SHAPE AND TRANSFER GENTLY TO FRYING PAN.
PUSH OUT: SIDES AND PULL UP EDGES OF DOUGH UNTIL YOU HAVE LINED ENTIRE INSIDE OF PAN.

THE FILLING

QUICHE IS BEST WHEN MADE IN THREE LAYERS:

LAYER ONE: SPREAD ONE CUP OF STIR FRIED VEGGIES ON THE BOTTOM OF THE CRUST. SUGGESTED VEGGIE COMBINATIONS — STIR FRIED ONIONS + BROCCOLI + PARSLEY + DILL; SPINACH + MUSHROOMS + OREGANO + CHOPPED WALNUTS; TOMATOES + GREEN PEPPERS; CAULIFLOWER + SHREDDED CARROT + CARAWAY.

LAYER TWO: GENEROUSLY BLANKET VEGGIES WITH ONE (OR MORE) CUP(S) OF CHEESE.

LAYER THREE: TOP VEGGIES AND CHEESE WITH THE FOLLOWING EGG-CUSTARD MIXTURE:

2 EGGS, BEATEN
1 CUP MILK   } MIX
1/2 t. SALT

FOR TOFU CUSTARD: SUBSTITUTE TOFU FOR 1 EGG. AND 1/2 CUP MILK

BAKE: IN COAL FIRE COVERED 30-40 MINUTES.

Foiled Food

IF YOU PLAN TO HAVE A FIRE, WHY NOT TRY PACKAGING YOUR FAVORITE INGREDIENTS IN HEAVY TIN FOIL AND BAKING THEM IN HOT COALS.

- LINE YOUR FIRE PIT WITH DRY STONES.
- COVER STONES WITH HOT COALS AND LET SIT FOR 10 MINUTES
- ADD FOIL WRAPPED FOOD AND COVER WITH MORE COALS

SOME IDEAS FOR FOIL DINNERS:

FOIL-BAKED FISH

- LAY OUT FISH ON FOIL AND BUTTER GENEROUSLY
- SPRINKLE WITH SEASONINGS (CURRY POWDER, CUMIN, MUSTARD CELERY SEED AND PARSLEY ARE GOOD!)
- COVER WITH ANY OF THE FOLLOWING: CHOPPED ONION, CELERY, TOMATO SLICES, DICED APPLES OR PINEAPPLE
- SEAL TIGHTLY WITH FOIL AND PLACE ON COALS
- BAKE 20-30 MINUTES, FISH WILL FLAKE WHEN DONE.

FOILED VEGGIES

- DICE 2 CARROTS, 2 POTATOES, 1 ONION, 1 GREEN PEPPER AND HANDFUL NUTS
- PLACE ON BUTTERED FOIL AND ADD 4 T WATER, DASH SOY SAUCE, PARSLEY OR ROSEMARY.
- SEAL AND BAKE 20 MINUTES
- SERVE TOPPED WITH GRATED CHEESE

SIMPLE TREATS for the Sweet Tooth

Apple Crisp
serves 4-5

4 DICED APPLES
1 C. GRAPE NUTS
1 C. RAISINS
1/2 C. BOILING WATER
2-3 T BUTTER
1/4 C. HONEY
CINNAMON, NUTMEG TO TASTE

COOK: APPLES IN BOILING WATER, TURN TO SIMMER AFTER 2-3 MINUTES
ADD: HONEY, BUTTER, RAISINS AND SPICES UNTIL WELL ABSORBED IN APPLES.
MIX IN: GRAPE NUTS AND SIMMER
TOP: WITH YOGURT OR ICE CREAM

Vanilla-Honey Custard
serves 6

4 C. MILK
4-6 EGGS, BEATEN WELL
1/4 C. HONEY
1/4 C. RAISINS
3 t. VANILLA
PINCH SALT

MIX: INGREDIENTS IN SAUCEPAN.
COOK: OVER MEDIUM HEAT AND STIR CONSTANTLY UNTIL CUSTARD COATS SPOON. DO NOT ALLOW TO BOIL.
REMOVE: FROM HEAT AND STIR IN VANILLA

Banana Fritters
serves 8

3 T. FLOUR
2 T. CORNSTARCH
1 T. SUGAR OR HONEY
1/2 C. MILK
1 EGG, BEATEN
1/8 t. BAKING POWDER
1 T. BUTTER, SOFTENED
8 BANANAS, sliced length-wise
2 T OIL

COMBINE: FIRST FOUR INGREDIENTS
STIR NEXT THREE INGREDIENTS
DIP: BANANA SLICES IN MIXTURE AND BROWN IN PREHEATED OIL.

Creamy Rice Pudding

1 C. MILK
1/8 t. SALT
1 C. RAW RICE
1/4 C. RAISINS
1/4 C. WALNUTS (OPTIONAL)
2 EGGS, SLIGHTLY BEATEN
1 t. VANILLA
1/4 C. HONEY
  DASH NUTMEG, CINNAMON.

HEAT: MILK AND SALT OVER MEDIUM
        FLAME UNTIL WARM
STIR IN: RICE, BOIL, THEN TURN TO
        SIMMER
ADD: RAISINS, NUTS AND COOK UNTIL
        RICE IS DONE. ADD SPICES
COMBINE: EGG, HONEY AND VANILLA,
        AND ADD TO RICE MIXTURE
STIR: AND COOK UNTIL RICE THICKENS.

Peanut-Chocolate Delight

CHUNKY PEANUT BUTTER
SEMI-SWEET CHOCOLATE CHIPS
RAISINS
GRAHAM CRACKERS

SPREAD: PEANUT BUTTER ON 2
        GRAHAM CRACKERS
PLACE: CHOCOLATE CHIPS AND
        RAISINS ON ONE SIDE
MAKE: A SANDWICH AND WARM
        SLOWLY IN A FRY PAN
        OR EAT IMMEDIATELY

P.B. BALLS

1/2 C. HONEY
1/2 C. PEANUT BUTTER
1/2 C. SUNFLOWER SEEDS
3/4 C. WHEAT GERM
3/4 C. MILK POWDER
1/2 C. RAISINS

MIX: ALL INGREDIENTS
ROLL: INTO BALLS
WATCH: DISAPPEAR!

FRUIT (DRIED OR FRESH)
CINNAMON, NUTMEG AND GINGER
BUTTER
ICE CREAM

MIX: 1/2 C. PER PERSON WITH
        1/4 to 1/2 C. WATER
ADD: 1/2 t. CINNAMON, PINCH
        NUTMEG AND GINGER
SIMMER: IN PAN UNTIL FRUIT
        IS TENDER
ADD: 2 T BUTTER AND ALLOW
        TO MELT
TOP: WITH ICE CREAM OR
        YOGURT

BEFORE YOU BEGIN YOUR CYCLING ADVENTURE, TAKE ADVANTAGE OF THE LUXURY OF YOUR KITCHEN STOVE BY BAKING A BATCH OF BAR COOKIES OR GRANOLA THAT YOU CAN CARRY WITH YOU ON THE ROAD. ALTHOUGH THEY MIGHT BE GOBBLED UP QUICKLY, THESE TREATS WILL PROVIDE MORE FUEL AND NUTRIENTS THAN YOUR AVERAGE SNACK.

CARROT BARS

PEANUT BUTTER BARS

½ C. PEANUT BUTTER
½ C. BUTTER OR MARGARINE
1 C. HONEY
1 C. SUNFLOWER SEEDS
1 C. WHOLE WHEAT FLOUR
1 C. WHEAT GERM
⅓ C. POWDERED MILK (INSTANT)
½ C. RAISINS
½ C. COCONUT
1 t. SALT
2 t. BAKING POWDER

MIX: PEANUT BUTTER, BUTTER AND HONEY
BEAT IN: EGGS
STIR TOGETHER: WHOLE WHEAT FLOUR, WHEAT GERM, DRY MILK, RAISINS, COCONUT, SALT AND BAKING POWDER.
ADD: DRY MIXTURE TO BATTER AND STIR WELL.
SPOON: BATTER INTO 13½" X 9½" PAN.
BAKE: AT 350° FOR 25 MINUTES
makes 25 bars

½ C. BUTTER OR MARGARINE
½ C. HONEY
2 EGGS
1 C. WHOLE WHEAT FLOUR
1 C. WHEAT GERM
1 t. BAKING POWDER
½ t. SALT
½ t. CINNAMON
⅛ t. CLOVES
1 C. GRATED, RAW CARROTS
1 C. SEEDLESS RAISINS
¼ C. PEANUT BUTTER.

MIX WELL: BUTTER AND HONEY
ADD: EGGS, MIX WELL
COMBINE SEPARATELY: FLOUR, BAKING POWDER, SALT, SPICES; STIR INTO BATTER.
ADD: CARROTS, RAISINS, PEANUT BUTTER.
SPOON: BATTER INTO GREASED 13½" X 9½" PAN.
BAKE: AT 350° FOR 25 to 30 MINUTES.
MAKES 42 BARS

POPCORN

FEW FOODS HAVE GAINED SUCH WIDESPREAD APPEAL AS THE SIMPLE, YET EXPLOSIVE SNACK FOOD KNOWN AS POPCORN. ITS AIRY MYSTIQUE UNMISTAKABLE FLAVOR AND CURIOUS SHAPE HAS RESULTED IN INCURABLE ADDICTIONS. ANXIOUSLY I LISTEN TO THE BOMBARDING KERNELS AWAITING THE MOMENT WHEN I CAN GRIP MY FINGERS AROUND THE PUFFED MORSELS AND FINALLY STUFF A HANDFUL AWKWARDLY INTO MY MOUTH.

THE DELICATE FLAVOR OF POPCORN CAN BE EASILY DESTROYED BY BURNING OR OVERSALTING. AFTER MANY YEARS OF POPPING, I HAVE FOUND THE FOLLOWING METHOD MOST SUCCESSFUL:

COAT THE BOTTOM OF A LARGE POT <u>GENEROUSLY</u> WITH OIL. PLACE ON HEAT AND DROP ONE DEFENSELESS KERNEL INTO THE OIL. WHEN IT POPS, IT IS JUST THE RIGHT TEMPERATURE TO ADD MORE KERNELS. ADD ONLY ENOUGH TO LAYER THE BOTTOM ONE KERNEL THICK. REPLACE THE LID AND WAIT PATIENTLY. WHEN THE POPPING SUBSIDES, LET OUT A LITTLE STEAM OR SHAKE THE POT AND REPLACE ON HEAT UNTIL POPPING STOPS — IMMEDIATELY REMOVE FROM HEAT AND ENJOY IT PERFECTLY PLAIN OR COATED WITH ANY OF THE FOLLOWING:

- MELTED BUTTER AND SALT
- BREWER'S YEAST
- PARMESAN CHEESE
- FEW TEASPOONS SOY SAUCE
- PALOMITAS MEXICANAS (MEXICAN POPCORN)
    BUTTER MELTED WITH A FEW DASHES
    CHILI POWDER, GARLIC, CUMIN, AND
    BLACK PEPPER
- HERBED POPCORN: BUTTER MELTED WITH
    LOTS OF OREGANO, BASIL AND PARSLEY
- BUTTER MELTED WITH GARLIC AND ONION
                              POWDER
- 2 PARTS BUTTER MELTED WITH ONE
    PART HONEY OR MAPLE SYRUP
- 3 PARTS BUTTER MELTED WITH ONE
    PART ORANGE JUICE AND DASH CINNAMON
- 3 PARTS BUTTER MELTED WITH ONE
    PART PEANUT BUTTER

Hot Drinks

WHEN THE AIR IS CHILLY EARLY IN THE MORNING OR AFTER SUNDOWN, THERE IS NOTHING LIKE WARMING YOUR HANDS AND YOUR INSIDES WITH A HOT DRINK. HOT DRINKS ARE ALSO A GOOD WAY TO REPLACE THE FLUIDS LOST DURING A WHOLE DAY OF CYCLING.

CAMP CAFÉ makes 4 cups

3 C. WATER
4 HANDFULS GROUNDS

BOIL: WATER
ADD : GROUNDS AND HEAT (DO NOT BOIL) GROUNDS. COFFEE IS DONE WHEN GROUNDS SINK WHEN POT IS TAPPED LIGHTLY.

CAFÉ MOCHA

1 PART COCOA
3 PARTS HOT COFFEE
1 PART POWDERED MILK

HOT MULLED CIDER makes 4 cups

1 QT. APPLE CIDER
2 T CINNAMON
1 t. CLOVES
1 ORANGE DICED
1 T. BUTTER OR MARGARINE.

COMBINE: ALL INGREDIENTS IN A PAN
HEAT : UNTIL BOILING, ALLOW THE MIXTURE TO SIT AND BLEND FLAVORS

STEAMING FRUIT

makes approximately 10 cups

1 lb. DRIED FRUIT
1½ Qt. WATER
1/2 C. HONEY OR TO TASTE
2 T. CINNAMON
1 T. CLOVE
3 ORANGES SLICED
1/2 GALLON CIDER

COOK: DRIED FRUIT WITH WATER FOR 15 MINUTES
ADD: REMAINING INGREDIENTS AND HEAT 15 MORE MINUTES.

CRANBERRY PUNCH

makes aproximately 6 cups

4 C. WATER
4 C. CRANBERRIES
HONEY TO TASTE
3 t. CINNAMON
3 t. CLOVES
ORANGE OR APPLE SLICES.

COOK: CRANBERRIES IN WATER UNTIL THE SKIN POPS OPEN.
DRAIN: LIQUID INTO SMALL POT
BOIL : JUICE AND ADD REMAINING INGREDIENTS, STIR AND SERVE.

✳ APPENDIX ✳

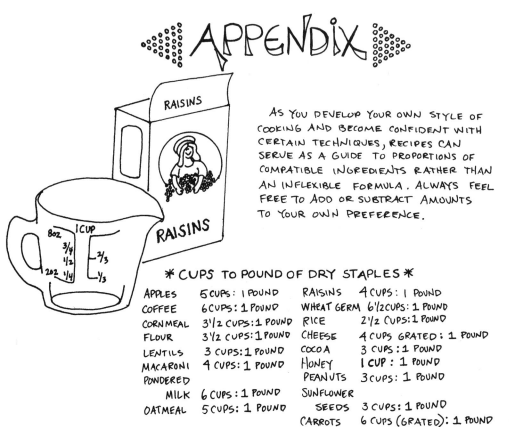

As you develop your own style of cooking and become confident with certain techniques, recipes can serve as a guide to proportions of compatible ingredients rather than an inflexible formula. Always feel free to add or subtract amounts to your own preference.

✳ CUPS TO POUND OF DRY STAPLES ✳

APPLES	5 CUPS : 1 POUND	RAISINS	4 CUPS : 1 POUND
COFFEE	6 CUPS : 1 POUND	WHEAT GERM	6½ CUPS : 1 POUND
CORN MEAL	3½ CUPS : 1 POUND	RICE	2½ CUPS : 1 POUND
FLOUR	3½ CUPS : 1 POUND	CHEESE	4 CUPS GRATED : 1 POUND
LENTILS	3 CUPS : 1 POUND	COCOA	3 CUPS : 1 POUND
MACARONI	4 CUPS : 1 POUND	HONEY	1 CUP : 1 POUND
POWDERED MILK	6 CUPS : 1 POUND	PEANUTS	3 CUPS : 1 POUND
OATMEAL	5 CUPS : 1 POUND	SUNFLOWER SEEDS	3 CUPS : 1 POUND
		CARROTS	6 CUPS (GRATED) : 1 POUND

✳ COOKING CHART FOR BEANS AND GRAINS ✳

PER 1 CUP DRY	ADD WATER	COVER AND SIMMER
BARLEY	2½ CUPS	1 HOUR
MILLET	3½ CUPS	30 MINUTES
OAT FLAKES (WHOLE)	3 CUPS	30 MINUTES
(QUICK)	3 CUPS	3 MINUTES
RICE SHORT GRAIN	2½ CUPS	50 MINUTES
LONG GRAIN	1½ CUPS	45 MINUTES
CRACKED WHEAT	3 CUPS	20 MINUTES
CHICK PEAS (SOAK 3 HRS)	4 CUPS	2-3 HOURS
LENTILS	3 CUPS	1 HOUR
SOYBEANS (SOAK 3 HRS)	4 CUPS	3-4 HOURS
SPLIT PEAS (SOAK 1 HR.)	3 CUPS	45 MINUTES
SOY FLAKES	2 CUPS	1-2 HOURS.

84.

EQUIVALENTS and SUBSTITUTIONS

1 C. FRESH MILK	=	4 T. POWDERED + 1 C. WATER
1 C. FRESH MILK	=	1/2 C. EVAPORATED MILK + 1/2 C. WATER
CAN OF CREAM SOUP	=	2 T FLOUR MIXED IN 6 OZ. COLD WATER HEATED AND MIXED WITH 2 BOUILLON CUBES.
1 T. CORNSTARCH	=	2 T FLOUR
1 C. SUGAR	=	1/2 C. HONEY BUT REDUCE LIQUID OF RECIPE BY 1/4 CUP
MOST DRIED HERBS	=	3 - 4 TIMES AS MUCH FRESH HERBS.
1 C. CANNED TOMATOES	=	1 - 3 FRESH TOMATOES, CHOPPED

t. = TEASPOON		3 t = 1 T	= 1 oz
T = TABLESPOON		4 T = 1/4 C	= 2 oz
C = CUP		8 FLUID OZ.	= 1 C.
lb = POUND		16 oz	= 1 lb.
oz = OUNCE		28.5 gr	= 1 oz
Pt = PINT		2 C.	= 1 PINT
Qt = QUART		4 C.	= 1 QUART
GAL. = GALLON		4 Qt	= 1 GALLON.

EQUIPMENT SUPPLIERS

GREAT WORLD WILDERNESS OUTFITTERS
250 FARMS VILLAGE ROAD
WEST SIMSBURY, CONN. 06092

RECREATIONAL EQUIPMENT INC (R.E.I.)
P.O. BOX C-88125
SEATTLE, WASH.

EASTERN MOUNTAIN SPORTS (EMS)
VOSE FARM ROAD
PETERBOROUGH, N.H. 03458

BIKE WAREHOUSE
8063 SOUTHERN BLVD.
YOUNGSTOWN, OHIO 44512

BIKECOLOGY BIKE SHOPS
P.O. BOX 66-909
DEPT. B-10
LOS ANGELES, CALIF.
90066

Completing the Cycle

AFTER EXPERIMENTING WITH SOME OF THE RECIPES FROM THIS LITTLE COOKBOOK, THE QUESTION ARISES — IS YOUR INNER TUBE SATISFIED? HOPEFULLY YOUR REPLY WILL BE "ONLY TEMPORARILY." FOR IF I HAVE REALLY SUCCEEDED IN WHETTING YOUR APPETITE FOR GOOD FOOD, THEN YOUR CONCOCTIONS WILL NOT BE LIMITED TO THE RECIPES IN THIS BOOK.

WHEN IT COMES TO CYCLING AND COOKING, SATISFACTION IS ALWAYS A TRANSITORY STATE OF MIND. FOR EVERY TIME WE FINISH A FULL DAY OF JOURNEYING, THEN COOK AND EAT A DELICIOUS MEAL, AND FINALLY LIE NUMB IN OUR SACKS, WE FEEL "SATISFIED." YET SIMULTANEOUSLY CRAVE TO DO IT ALL OVER AGAIN.

IF YOUR GOAL WHILE TOURING IS TO FEEL UNITED WITH YOUR BICYCLE, THE LANDSCAPE, YOUR COMPANIONS, AND THE FOOD THAT SUSTAINS YOU, SATISFACTION DOES NOT MERELY SIGNAL AN END TO YOUR EFFORTS, BUT RATHER IT BECOMES A PERPETUAL IMPETUS THROUGHOUT YOUR TRAVELS.

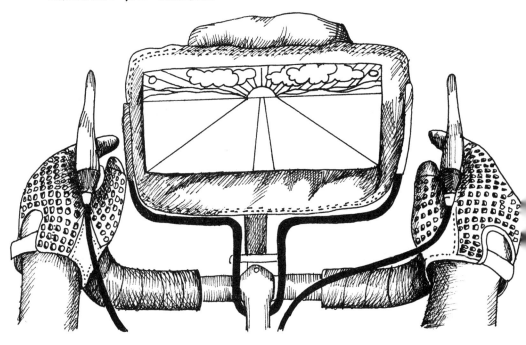

BICYCLE BIBLIOGRAPHY

BALLANTINE, RICHARD, RICHARD'S BICYCLE BOOK, BALLANTINE BOOKS, N.Y. N.Y., 1976

BRIDGE, RAYMOND, FREEWHEELING, THE BICYCLE CAMPING BOOK, STACKPOLE BOOKS, HARRISBURG, P.A., 1974.

CUTHBERTSON, TOM, ANYBODY'S BIKE BOOK, 1979
          BIKE TRIPPING, 1972, TEN SPEED PRESS, BERKELY, CALIF.

DELONG, FRED, DELONG'S GUIDE TO BICYCLES AND BICYCLING, CHILTON BOOK COMPANY, RADNOR, PA.

GLEN, HOWARD, GLEN'S COMPLETE BICYCLE MANUAL, CROWN PUBLISHERS, N.Y, 1973

HAWKINS, GARY AND KAREN, BICYCLE TOURING IN EUROPE, PANTHEON BOOKS, N.Y., N.Y., 1980

RAKOWSKI, JOHN, COOKING ON THE ROAD, ANDERSON WORLD INC. MOUNTAIN VIEW, CALIF., 1980

OTHER BOOKS OF INTEREST

BARKER, HARRIET, THE ONE-BURNER GOURMET, CONTEMPORARY BOOKS, CHICAGO, ILL, 1981

CLARK, NANCY, THE ATHLETE'S KITCHEN, CBI PUBLISHING COMPANY, BOSTON, MASS, 1981

EWALD, ELLEN BUCHMAN, RECIPES FOR A SMALL PLANET, BALLANTINE BOOKS, N.Y, N.Y., 1975

FLEMING, JUNE, THE WELL-FED BACKPACKER, VICTORIA HOUSE, PORTLAND, OR, 1979

MILLER, DORIS, THE NEW HEALTHY TRAIL FOOD BOOK, EAST WOODS PRESS, CHARLOTTE, N.C., 1980

THE NATIONAL OUTDOOR LEADERSHIP SCHOOL, NOLS COOKERY, EMPORIA STATE PRESS, EMPORIA, KANSAS.

PETZOLD, PAUL, THE WILDERNESS HANDBOOK, W.W. NORTON AND COMPANY INC. N.Y, N.Y., 1977